Universal Design Ideas for Style, Comfort & Safety

RSMeans

Reed Construction Data®

Copyright © 2007
Reed Construction Data, Inc.
Construction Publishers & Consultants
63 Smiths Lane
Kingston, MA 02364-3008
781-422-5000
www.rsmeans.com
RS**Means** is a product line of Reed Construction Data.

RSMeans Managing Editor: Mary Greene. Editor: Andrea Sillah.
Editorial Assistant: Jessica deMartin. Production Manager: Michael Kokernak.
Cover design: Norman R. Forgit.

Designed and Produced by Lexicon Consulting, Inc.
300 East Locust, Suite 230
Des Moines, IA 50309
www.lexiconconsultinginc.com
515-243-4615

Executive Director: Catherine M. Staub, Ed.D. Managing Editor: Julie Collins.
Associate Editor: Katie Stuler. Graphic Designer: James A. Stepp.
Associate Graphic Designer: Holly Reynolds. Photography: James A. Stepp.
Illustration: Holly Reynolds. Editorial & Design Intern: Randall Noblet.

Cover photographs
Main photograph: Copyright Armstrong World Industries, Inc., Interior Design: Larry Burns Design, Lancaster, PA
Left and center insets: Copyright Bob Greenspan, courtesy of Mascord
Right inset: Copyright Progress Lighting

Printed in the United States of America

10 9 8 7 6 5 4 3 2 1

Library of Congress Number Pending

ISBN 978-0-87629-091-0

Universal Design Ideas
for Style, Comfort & Safety

Your Dream Home, Forever

For many homeowners, creating a place that's safe, easy to access, and comfortable is a priority. This is where universal design comes in. Perhaps you're remodeling or building the home you plan to live in for the next few years—or for the rest of your life. Implementing universal design from the beginning of the process will save you money and give you the best result. Come along as we show you how to make design-for-all concepts an integral part of your dream home.

Design Basics

Universal design helps you create an accessible and beautiful home. Its features can be invisible while adding safety, comfort, and value. The result? A home you can enjoy now and for years to come.

This book was written to provide inspiration and ideas on how to implement universal design into your residence from the beginning of the building or remodeling process. The results are beautiful and functional—and will accommodate accessibility needs if and when they arise.

Each chapter provides an overview of what can be done to make individual portions of your home—from the entry through each room in the house to the backyard—as usable as possible for every person who enters, regardless of age, height, weight, and physical ability. The information presented includes general design ideas, material recommendations, and accessibility guidelines culled from expert interviews and sources including the AARP, National Kitchen and Bath Association (NKBA), National Association of Home Builders (NAHB) 50+ Housing Council, The Center for Universal Design, and more. (For a complete list of sources, see pages 154–155.)

The key is to remember that recommendations are just that. Take some; leave some. It's all about creating a home that you like, that you can use comfortably, that you want to be in—a home that reflects your personal requirements, preferences, and interests. If you have space, widen the doorways as much as or more than recommended or allow extra room between bathroom fixtures. Is your kitchen floor plan tight, with no room to expand? Then skip the space recommendations and focus on functionality. Do what makes sense for your space, budget, and needs.

Proper placement of kitchen appliances, furniture, and other items ensures that people of all ages and physical abilities can navigate a universally designed home with ease.

Photo courtesy of Armstrong World Industries, Inc.

What is Universal Design?

Ron Mace, founder of The Center for Universal Design at North Carolina State University, coined the term "universal design" to describe the concept of designing products and environments to be attractive and usable by everyone to the greatest extent possible—regardless of age or ability. A number of other terms are synonymous with universal design—*design for all, inclusive design, transgenerational design,* and *lifespan design.* No matter what it's called, however, the ultimate goal is the same.

James Joseph Pirkl, FIDSA, professor emeritus at Syracuse University and founding director of Transgenerational Design Matters, Inc., points to the universality of the approach: "Transgenerational design accommodates, and appeals to, people of all ages and abilities: the young, the old, the able, the disabled—without

Welcoming visitors to your universally designed home may involve ushering them from a stair-free walkway to a door beneath an overhang that protects them from the elements. A no-threshold entrance would make this area even more user-friendly.

penalty to any group. A transgenerational house is a human-centered house. It's not about building specialized 'elderly' housing or just providing 'adaptive' products like grab bars, lever door handles, and toilet seat raisers. It is about designing residential environments and household products that accommodate and benefit the widest market segments without penalty to any group."

Mary Jo Peterson, a certified kitchen and bath designer, aging-in-place specialist, and active adult specialist in housing, agrees: "When I explain universal design, I talk about designing the space so that it will support and enhance the life of whoever lives in it for the life of the house, because needs in the household and demands on the house change over time, and the people who live in and visit the house change over time."

Experts who promote universal design stress that it's about more than standards and accessibility codes. "Universal design unites health care, design, production, and building professionals to create products and environments that accommodate human functional diversity and changes that occur secondary to illness, injury, and aging," says Susan Mack, president of Homes for Easy Living Universal Design Consultants, a certified aging-in-place specialist, and a licensed occupational therapist. "It enhances quality of life for people of all ages and abilities by improving safety, ergonomics, and work efficiency."

Accessible vs. Universal

Some universal design experts draw a line between the terms "accessible design" and "universal design." Why?

"Accessible design features are a part of universal design. However, universal design is much more," says expert Susan Mack. "Universal design goes beyond the minimum standards required by accessibility codes and seeks to create the best functional results, rather than just the minimum." Mack emphasizes that universal design benefits all people—not just those who may have a disability.

One example: Not everyone wants (or needs) a grab bar on the wall next to the toilet, a common requirement in accessibility codes. But in a universally designed home, the reinforcement or backing is installed within the wall during construction, even if the actual grab bar isn't. That way, it's easy to add a support bar if someone in the home needs one later. "Being readily adaptable is an important aspect of universal design," Mack says.

Because the term "accessible design" does not encompass everything universal design does, you won't find those terms used synonymously in this book. But you will see the word "accessible" used in the general sense, because much of what is discussed in the following chapters does, in fact, make a home easier to access for residents and visitors alike.

Placement of kitchen elements may not be convenient for cooks whose heights, sizes, and strengths may vary from what builders consider "standard." This contemporary kitchen is one example of a design that keeps everything within easy reach of the cook.

Why Universal Design?

"Shouldn't a kitchen, bath, laundry, or patio be as readily used by a child, a teenager with a broken arm, a baby boomer with heart disease, an older adult with arthritis, or a pregnant woman?" asks James Joseph Pirkl, FIDSA.

Universal design doesn't just make a home livable for wheelchair users or the elderly. It makes life easier for everyone, from the moment they enter your home until they leave. Even if members of your family are perfectly healthy and agile now, a future injury or a more permanent disability can leave them struggling to get around the house. This type of design helps people with temporary or long-term disabilities—from an injured hand to a bad back—enjoy life in their homes.

Healthy, able individuals can also benefit from universal design. Sure, the single-lever faucets recommended for use in kitchens and baths make it easier for people who have limited hand strength or an injury to turn the faucet on and

Aging in Place

Today, Americans are staying in their homes longer than ever before. Yet even as we're remaining active and living longer, physical changes are inevitable. That means the two-story house that works for a thirty-something couple raising children may not cut it once that couple reaches retirement.

"As we age, we can anticipate one or more physical and sensory impairments, such as heart disease, stroke, arthritis, diabetes, and declining eyesight and hearing," says James Joseph Pirkl, FIDSA. At the same time in your life that you're trying to eat well and exercise regularly to minimize your chances of acquiring such impairments, you can be creating a house that's livable should they occur. That's where universal design comes in. Regardless of how old you are when you remodel or build your home, transgenerational design can make your home livable for the long run by combining elements of safety, convenience, and comfort.

Good Grips®, Good Idea

For an example of the way products—and entire homes—can be attractive and easy for everyone to use, look no further than the utensil drawer in your kitchen.

The Oxo Good Grips line of kitchen utensils was introduced in 1990 for people who were limited by arthritis. These upscale products didn't look anything like their functional but not-so-pretty predecessors at the time—although they performed the same tasks. The products' attractive appearance (and profitability—Oxo International grew 40 to 50 percent a year between 1990 and 1995 as sales jumped to $20 million a year) underscores the benefit of melding functionality with aesthetics in the home.

No one called the Good Grips line "accessible"—even though that's exactly what the products are.

"If manufacturers use stigmatizing terms that in effect are implying aging, disability, or impairment, people are going to reject the product," says James Joseph Pirkl, FIDSA. "If somebody is young and active and has all their capabilities, they are not going to automatically pay a premium for accessible design, unless the product is cool and desirable by all. This is why Oxo products have been so successful."

And this is what homebuilders, manufacturers, and homeowners are discovering: good universal design, which also is attractive home design, increases value and livability for everyone.

off. But they also help you to easily turn on the water when your hands are dirty and you don't want to grasp the faucet. Widened doorways allow people who use wheelchairs to travel through the house, but they also make it easier for parents carrying young children around or homeowners loaded down with groceries to enter and move around.

You may even have universal design elements in your home right now and not realize it. That's the key. Good universal design should be virtually invisible.

The design of products created to assist people in their homes has come a long way—these grab bars are as attractive as they are useful.

Photo © Brynn Bruijn Photography; courtesy of Great Grabz

Universal Design Basics

There are no set-in-stone rules when it comes to design-for-all principles. There are, however, a few overarching ideas worth noting, namely that universal design is all of the following:

Inclusive. "Universal design welcomes people of all ages and abilities," says expert Susan Mack. "No one is excluded from family gatherings because of unnecessary barriers and hazards."

The idea of inclusion sparked certified kitchen and bath designer Mary Jo Peterson's interest in universal design. "I started to see that the things I was doing for my clients with disabilities oftentimes are just better design for everybody. And tah-dah! That's universal design. I gave up the idea that design should be different for a person with a disability and decided that design should be more inclusive for all of us. It should look good and support a variety of lifestyles, abilities, sizes, and ages of people."

Preventive. "Universal design enhances safety by reducing unnecessary hazards," Mack says. Statistics underscore the importance of safety in the home: falls are the leading cause of injury-related deaths in people over the age of 65.

And safety is a concern for all ages—not just those who are past 65. The bathroom, in particular, is often the site of slips and falls because of the prevalence of wet surfaces and the agility required to climb in and out of the shower and tub. No-step entries in showers, grab bars, and slip-resistant flooring all help reduce these risks.

Ergonomic and Efficient. Incorporating the principles of ergonomics and work simplification into the design of a home enhances comfort and convenience and makes life easier. "As the average life expectancy increases, we need to protect our bodies from unnecessary repetitive stress," Mack says. "We are all looking for ways to make our lives easier. Universal design creates ergonomic and work-efficient products and homes to reduce the time and energy required to perform our tasks of daily living."

Cushiony flooring materials, such as cork, make it easier to stand for long periods of time—perfect for areas like the kitchen or laundry room. And raising the height of the dishwasher means less bending, reducing back strain while making loading and unloading more efficient. "It's rethinking," Peterson says. "Don't do things as you've always done them, but as you wish they could be."

Attractive. A major misconception attached to universal design is that it is solely for people who are elderly or for people with disabilities. It is often equated with "accessible design," which may be viewed as institutional, unattractive, and unappealing. But incorporating universal design principles doesn't mean sacrificing style.

"Universal/transgenerational solutions should create a supportive residential environment that does not look institutional or imply 'aging' or

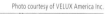

Photo courtesy of VELUX America Inc.

Good lighting—including a mix of natural and artificial light sources—is an important element of universal design in the kitchen and throughout the house.

Incorporating universal design principles can yield striking results. Here, an open floor plan, use of the same flooring from room to room, and glare-free lighting make the home more comfortable.

'disability,'" says James Joseph Pirkl, FIDSA. "The finished solution should look upbeat and attractive to young as well as older residents."

Adds Peterson: "I really don't think there are any hard-and-fast universal design rules, but if I were going to pick one, I would say if it doesn't look good, don't do it."

Transgenerational. Many households have three or more generations under one roof at one time or another. Universal design accommodates everyone—from grandchildren to grandparents. "Grandparents may be limiting their visitation with their children and grandchildren because a home isn't senior friendly," Mack says. "Universal design makes your home more welcoming."

Freedom of Choice

According to an AARP study, 83 percent of homeowners over age 45 want to stay in their current homes for the rest of their lives. "Universal design gives you freedom of choice to live where you want to live," says Susan Mack. "Unnecessary barriers and hazards in traditionally designed homes could force you into an institutional setting—or universal design can support your choice to 'age in place.'"

The baby-boomer generation is helping to revolutionize universal design and the way people think about aging in place. "As they're aging, they're going to be much more demanding of products and ways that their lives can be enhanced," says James Joseph Pirkl, FIDSA. "Manufacturers and home builders are beginning to understand where the baby boomers are coming from; instead of stigmatizing them, they're acknowledging the fact that they're growing old but continue to be active, and they are going to supply them with houses that will allow them to continue to live their lifestyles." He adds that this type of design promotes and extends independence, removes barriers, offers greater choices, and enhances quality of life for any group—which is the essence of transgenerational design.

Next Steps

Once you've read the following chapters, which discuss specifics for each area of a home, you may be wondering how to go about implementing design-for-all ideas. In this book, mark the pages that have ideas you like and then check the resources and credits on pages 154–157. There you'll find contact information for many of the products and materials featured. (Most are available through national retailers. A few are specialty items with more limited availability.) Then expand your search to the Internet and/or magazines, creating a clipping file of product ideas to build on your "wish list." Seek advice from seasoned professionals and organizations, such as AARP, the National Association of Home Builders, and The Center for Universal Design. (You'll find contact information for these and other organizations on pages 154–155.)

Texture, color, and contrast are important considerations with universal design. In this bedroom, the furniture contrasts with the subtle colors and soft fabrics.

Money Matters

Many universal design features—such as positioning outlets and switches properly—have zero added cost if they are incorporated correctly into new construction. Implementing other universal design dimensions, materials, and recommendations at the beginning of the process may cost 2 to 4 percent more. It pays to spend a little more money up-front, however, because modifying an existing home later can cost as much as 30 percent more. And some modifications, such as those to corridors, stairways, and doorways, may not be possible later, depending on the size and layout of your home. At the end of each chapter in this book, you'll find some project examples with costs, which can give you some basic budget parameters.

Photo courtesy of Dunn-Edwards Corporation

Photo © Jupiterimages

Backyards benefit from universal design, too. Level patio surfaces, plenty of open space around furnishings, and the right amount of shade help make outdoor living comfortable.

It also pays to consult with a specialist who has a proven track record of success in universal design. "Currently, there is no required certification for universal design consultants," says expert Susan Mack. But you can find quality professionals with expertise in this area. "It's important to hire a universal design consultant with years of experience in designing for people of all ages and abilities, because the best choices are based on a depth of knowledge of human function and not just on the minimum required by statutes," Mack adds. Learn more about working with professionals on page 148.

The Principles of Universal Design

The Center for Universal Design enlisted the help of a group of architects, product designers, engineers, and environmental design researchers to create these seven principles of universal design.

1. Equitable Use. The design is useful and marketable to people with diverse abilities.

2. Flexibility in Use. The design accommodates a wide range of individual preferences and abilities.

3. Simple and Intuitive Use. Use of the design is easy to understand, regardless of the user's experience, knowledge, language skills, or current concentration level.

4. Perceptible Information. The design communicates necessary information effectively to the user, regardless of ambient conditions or the user's sensory abilities.

5. Tolerance for Error. The design minimizes hazards and the adverse consequences of accidental or unintended actions.

6. Low Physical Effort. The design can be used efficiently and comfortably, with a minimum of fatigue.

7. Size and Space for Approach and Use. Appropriate size and space is provided for approach, reach, manipulation, and use, regardless of the user's body size, posture, or mobility.

The Principles of Universal Design were conceived and developed by The Center for Universal Design at North Carolina State University. Use or application of the Principles in any form by an individual or organization is separate and distinct from the Principles and does not constitute or imply acceptance or endorsement by The Center for Universal Design of the use or application. Reproduced with permission from The Center for Universal Design.

2

Entrances & Floor Plans

It's easy to spot a house that has curb appeal—well-placed plantings and an attractive entry beckon. But can you tell you're entering a universally designed house before you reach the front door? Not if it's done right. Visitors will be drawn to your home because it's welcoming and attractive. The fact that it's easy for people to come and go will make them feel even more welcome.

Entrances

Creating a universally designed home begins before you even reach the front door. Eliminate the first barrier to your home by designing a walkway and front entry that are easily navigable for family members and visitors alike.

It's easy to overlook the exterior and entrances of your home in the rush to ensure interior spaces are designed just the way you envisioned them. But taking the time to plan for the proper exterior materials, pathways, and entrances is worthwhile so you know your home will be accessible and livable now and for years to come.

Walkways

Make the paths that lead to your house as safe as possible by installing a textured, nonslip, gently sloping concrete walkway at least 36 inches wide. A walkway that is 48 to 54 inches wide is even better because it allows people to walk side-by-side. Repair cracks and other damage as soon as they appear. To make pathways safer for walking year-round, you may wish to install an ice-thawing system beneath.

Exteriors

Are you prepared to undertake the ongoing maintenance many home exteriors require for the entire time you reside in your home? If not, consider installing low- or no-maintenance exterior materials, which can last the lifetime of your home and require minimal upkeep.

One popular, inexpensive option is vinyl siding, which won't rot or peel and can be selected to simulate wood. It's available seamed or seamless in a plethora of classic and modern colors; its solid coloration ensures scratches won't show. Metal siding—aluminum or steel—is available smoothed or embossed to

mimic wood grain in a variety of factory-baked enamel colors. Steel is not recommended in areas near saltwater or with heavy air pollution, but otherwise metal siding is a good choice that resists fire, rot, and insects. Another option: brick and stone veneers. Although they may be more expensive, they're beautiful, fireproof, and should last the life of your home.

Entrances

At least one entrance to your home should provide stair-free access. A no-step entrance makes it easier to carry belongings, push strollers or wheelchairs, or move furniture. In addition, avoiding steps reduces the possibility of falls. A no-step entrance does not necessarily mean installing a ramp to the front of your house—in fact, a gradual slope of 1:20 is best for connecting a walkway to the front porch or stoop. Just make certain the surface slopes away from the home to avoid moisture problems around the door.

If you love the curb appeal of your front entry and its not-so-accessible stairs, another option is to have a second entrance—perhaps easily

Photo © Bob Greenspan; courtesy of Mascord

Entryway lights don't have to be bright—in fact, 40- to 75-watt bulbs are all you need to create a beautifully illuminated entry.

A covered entry with a bench and well-placed lighting welcomes visitors. If a no-step front entry isn't a possibility, consider including another entry elsewhere that's more accessible.

Photo © Andersen Corporation

reached from a detached garage—without stairs. If you build a ramp, include a landing at the top and, if needed, the bottom; if the ramp is long, plan another landing in the middle or each time the ramp changes direction. Ramp safety precautions include making certain that the platform surface is level, that the ramp has no cross slope, that it won't become slippery when wet, and that guardrails and handrails are installed on both sides. Integrating a ramp with the architecture of your home ensures that it doesn't look like an afterthought. You can also purchase a removable wheelchair ramp for use when you have company.

At the front door, many elements recommended for creating a universal home also contribute to its curb appeal. A covered entrance provides protection from the elements when you are unlocking the door or greeting guests. To ensure house numbers are easy to spot, they should be in a large, simple typeface located about 60 inches above the floor on the latch side of the door. The doorbell or intercom should be located at an optimally usable height on the latch side of the door as well. Including a shelf or bench that is 10 to 12 inches wide provides a spot to place packages or other items while you open the door. At the door, make the threshold as flat as possible so guests can enter easily without tripping. A front door at least 36 inches wide is easiest to use. These recommendations and others for front entrances are available from the Iowa State University Housing Extension website (www.extension.iastate.edu/housing).

Exterior Lighting

For almost as long as electricity has been available, Americans have left a porch light on to welcome guests to their homes. Lighting walkways and entryways is important for safely guiding visitors to your house and improving nighttime security. A smart exterior lighting system illuminates the following:

- **Driveways.** Mount a motion-sensor downlight above the garage door. Path lights can be used to help define the edges of steep or winding driveways.

- **Pathways.** "You want people to feel safe as they are walking," says Eunice Noell-Waggoner, L.C., President of the Center of Design for an Aging Society. "Think of the path people will take and provide lighting along the way." Small, low-voltage lights mounted alongside a walkway show visitors where to step. This type of lighting should shine down to illuminate the path, not up into visitors' eyes. Provide additional lighting to illuminate any abrupt elevation changes.

- **Entryways.** Light fixtures at the front door should always be mounted above eye level and covered to minimize glare. "Exposed bulbs outside the home are bright and the glare they produce can have a blinding effect on a person walking up," Noell-Waggoner says. She recommends illuminating the entry with several fixtures rather than one high-wattage bulb. Sconces mounted on each side of the door or a pendant lantern hanging from the porch ceiling are common options. You also may want to illuminate your house numbers so they're visible from the street; a lighted doorbell and concentrated light on the door handle and lockset are also recommended.

- **Perimeter Areas.** Lighting around the perimeter of the house is a smart security move. Install spotlights directed at the walls, in dark corners, and around garages. Installing recessed lights in the underside of your eaves or roof overhang is another way to subtly light your home's exterior.

Floor Plan Basics

Before you begin building or remodeling, consider how you would like each room to function. An open floor plan is a must when creating universally designed spaces.

Introducing your guests to a beautiful, universally designed home begins in the entryway, but before you put out the welcome mat, you'll want to ensure that the rest of your home is easy to navigate as well. As you design your floor plan, remember that large, open rooms facilitate movement for people of all ages and ability levels. Minimize the number of walls and other barriers, and you'll be well on your way to creating accessible living spaces with style.

Entryways

Include wide doorways (at least 32 inches, preferably 36 inches) at the entrance. Allow for at least two feet of open floor space on the latch side of the door so there's plenty of room to approach it. A 5x5-foot maneuvering space inside and outside the main entrance ensures people on foot or in a wheelchair have the room they need.

A no-threshold front entry and consistent use of flooring between rooms help people move through a home easily.

Photo © Bob Greenspan; courtesy of Mascord

Photo © Andersen Corporation

If possible, plan for wide doorways and lots of natural light in your home.

Inside the house, provide a closet or cupboard for shoes and hooks for hanging jackets, purses, and other personal items. If possible, hang a mirror nearby for people to check their appearance when entering the house.

Throughout the House

A truly livable home removes or minimizes common barriers, such as changes in flooring elevation, stairs, narrow doors and hallways, and rooms that don't have ample turning space.

Universal design experts tout the benefits of building single-level homes. But if you are adamant about having a two-story dwelling, include a bedroom and a full bath on the main floor as well, or consider a convertible floor plan that allows you to easily convert rooms (such as a den or office) currently on the main floor into a first-floor master suite later. Another option is to include an elevator or stairlift in your floor plan. (Learn more about these on page 25.)

Today's open floor plans lend themselves to universal design—in fact, the more open the floor plan, the better. When remodeling, you may want to remove non-load-bearing walls, expand the width of interior doorways, and include additional windows to make your home seem larger and brighter.

Addressing Usability

Universal design principles are best incorporated into your home when it is first built. Yet many homeowners wait to address issues until something—perhaps a sudden injury—forces them to make changes. At that point, remodeling or basic modifications are required.

"Incorporating the principles of universal design is most cost-efficient and effective when it's done at the beginning of the design process of a new home," says aging-in-place specialist Susan Mack. This way, the design is part of the home, rather than an afterthought. And you can think ahead; for example, roughing in the plumbing for a shower in a powder room makes it easier to convert that space to a full bath later.

However, "incorporating universal design when planning a major remodeling project can be beneficial as well," Mack says. Redoing certain rooms—perhaps creating a more functional work area in the kitchen, stealing space from a spare room to expand the size of the master bathroom, or widening doorways—can enhance usability. There are limitations to what you will be able to achieve, however. You may be able to remove or move some walls to open up rooms, but this may not be easy because some walls will be load-bearing.

Some modifications can be costly, time consuming, and difficult, so it's best to pinpoint exactly what you're looking for before beginning a project. When it comes to making modifications, swapping out surface materials, selecting new fixtures and appliances, and improving lighting are all adjustments that can be made to your home without major remodeling.

Doorways & Doors

In your universally designed home, make certain that doors are secure yet easy to open and that doorways are wide enough for everyone to comfortably pass through.

Wide doorways make it possible to move furniture in and out of the home, ensure that suitcases don't scrape door frames, and allow people who use wheelchairs and walkers to travel through with ease. As mentioned earlier, a minimum of 32 inches is recommended for door openings, while 36 inches is ideal. Minimize or eliminate thresholds where possible.

Entry Doors

Entry doors work hard—they must withstand weather extremes and possible intruders, while providing an attractive welcome to your home. As with your home's exterior siding and lighting options, you want a door that is as maintenance-free and durable as possible. Look for a door that complements your home's siding and windows for the most cohesive look.

Exterior doors made of wood are the most traditional, and their weight makes them a sturdy, secure choice. However, wood doors are more expensive than some other options and require periodic maintenance—such as refinishing the surface—to stay in shape. Fiberglass is sturdy, energy-efficient, and low-maintenance—and it's generally less expensive than wood. These scratch-resistant doors are good for entrances that lack overhangs, because they can withstand wind, rain, and UV rays better than other materials. Steel is the least

expensive material, and also requires little maintenance. Like fiberglass, steel doors boast energy-efficient foam core insulation. And because they're fully weatherstripped, they can withstand the elements.

A front entry door with an operable, hinged sidelight increases door width to as much as 50 inches and simplifies moving furniture and other items into your home.

Interior Doors

Inside the house, doors possess an aesthetic as well as practical value. They are key to a wall's composition and can serve as a focal point.

Photo © Andersen Corporation

A front door with sidelights and a transom provides a friendly welcome and maximum light in the entry.

Solid wood 34- or 36-inch interior doors are sturdy and provide unmatched soundproofing qualities. They're also the most expensive option. Because solid wood—such as oak and white pine—swells and shrinks as humidity fluctuates, proper installation is essential. Solid-core doors resemble their solid wood counterparts but lack the high price tag. These doors feature a wood fiber core, which provides better protection from the spread of fires than hollow-core doors. Lightweight hollow-core doors are the least expensive and can be made of an oak or birch veneer or hardboard. Hardboard varieties are the most durable and resist swelling and shrinking.

If you have standard doors in your home, you could install swing-away hinges to increase the open doorway width for easier access. Or use double, louvered, or folding doors. Pocket doors are a great universal design option because they require no threshold, are easy to open and close, and eliminate the need for as much as 8 to 10 square feet of door swing space. Pocket doors should be 32 to 36 inches wide.

Door Hardware

Selecting the right hardware is vital to ensure that people carrying an armful of groceries or

Photo courtesy of Smarthome

A touch pad lockset allows you to enter a personalized code to open your door rather than fumbling with keys. You can also create temporary codes for houseguests or other people who need access.

who have limited hand strength can easily open doors. Replace round doorknobs with lever handles wherever possible, since they are easier to operate. Ideally, the handles should be at least 5 inches long and no higher than 44 inches from the floor. To make access even easier, consider installing automatic door openers/closers for existing doors. This is particularly helpful if there isn't sufficient space for a person using a wheelchair to open the door. Or consider locking and unlocking entrance doors by remote control, touch pad, or another form of keyless entry system.

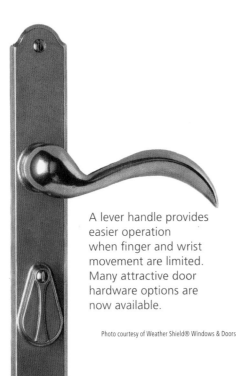

A lever handle provides easier operation when finger and wrist movement are limited. Many attractive door hardware options are now available.

Photo courtesy of Weather Shield® Windows & Doors

Safety Tip

Door and window security is vital in any home. To protect your home from forced entry, make sure all security mechanisms are burglar-proof but easy for you to unlock. Consider including two peepholes in exterior doors, with one lower for children or people who are seated. Sidelights and windows are attractive additions and provide another means of seeing who's outside. Cover them with sheer curtains for some privacy.

Flooring

Nonslip, level flooring should be a priority throughout your home to reduce the risk of slipping, tripping, or falling. There are plenty of beautiful, safe options.

If there's one thing that can't be stressed enough as you select the materials for your home, it's safe flooring. In addition to selecting nonslip flooring, limit the use of area rugs (or at least affix them to the floor with carpet tape) to prevent tripping. For added safety, you could consider installing tactile, high-contrast strips of a different texture on the floor to alert people with limited vision where flooring or elevation changes occur.

Flooring Options

Glazed ceramic tile, stone, vinyl flooring with a matte finish, and wood are all good flooring options. Although thick, plush carpet is comfortable underfoot, low-pile, tightly woven carpet is a more accessible option, particularly for homes where someone may be using a wheelchair or walker.

Two flooring options that are growing in popularity are cork and bamboo. Cork is recommended because of its naturally cushiony consistency, which makes it easier to stand for long periods of time. (Learn more on pages 42–43.) Bamboo flooring is a popular "green" option because, although it looks and feels like wood, bamboo is a grass that quickly replenishes itself, growing faster than trees. Bamboo is similar to wood in durability and comfort and is installed much like standard wood floors. (More information about flooring choices can be found throughout this book.)

Hickory plank flooring is one of many attractive flooring options.

Opt for the lowest threshold level possible—particularly when flooring materials change from room to room—to minimize the hazard of tripping.

Many universal homes limit walls and halls in favor of open rooms that flow into one another. If your new or remodeled home includes halls or passageways, try to make them wide and make sure they're well-lit.

Halls & Passageways

If eliminating hallways from your floor plan isn't an option, try to plan them to be 42 inches wide to ensure that they are easy to navigate. Including a 60-inch turning radius at the intersection of halls is another accommodation worth making, because it makes it easier to move items such as bicycles in and out of the home—plus it provides turnaround space for people who use wheelchairs. Angled doorways at least 36 inches wide help make it easier to enter rooms located on either side of the hallway. Just be sure to scale spaces properly so doorways and hallways are in proportion.

Lighting and Decor

Make sure hallways are safely illuminated. One ceiling fixture may suffice in a small hallway, while wall-mount sconces can help illuminate a longer one. Avoid over-lighting the hall, as too much light in such a confined area can create glare. For night lighting, consider low-level LED lights in the walls near the floor.

Photo courtesy of Armstrong World Industries, Inc.

Designing wide doorways and continuing the same flooring from the hallway to each room help make homes easier to navigate. Inlaid wood in a contrasting color visually separates the spaces.

Tubular skylights provide natural light in hallways but must be supplemented by other light sources.

Photo courtesy of VELUX America Inc.

Safety Tip

Using the same flooring throughout your living spaces and eliminating thresholds between rooms minimizes tripping hazards and makes it easier for people using wheelchairs or scooters to maneuver. If your flooring does change from room to room and thresholds are necessary, either recess the threshold or select square thresholds that are no higher than ¼ inch or slanted thresholds no taller than ½ inch. If your existing thresholds are higher than this, consider using transition wedges.

Stairs

Ideally, your home's main activity areas will be reachable without stairs. If you live in a multi-story home, look for ways to make your stairs easier to use.

Universally designed homes function best when all of the living areas, including bedrooms and baths, are located on one level. If your home has stairs, these guidelines will help make them easier to use.

Staircase Safety

To make your staircases as accessible as possible, include a few key safety precautions (many of which are required by building codes). All steps should be constructed of or covered with a nonslip surface. And every stairway that has two or more steps should include a sturdy handrail. Where possible, mount a rail on each side of the stairwell; for additional support, extend the rails 12 inches past the top and bottom steps. Handrails attached to the wall should be tightly screwed into studs so they

can support up to 250 pounds of weight. Position handrails 34 inches from the floor and 1½ inches from the wall.

Stairways should be well-lit, with light switches at the top and bottom. Motion-detector lights ensure that stairs are illuminated even if you forget to flip the light switch. In addition to overhead lights or wall sconces, small lights in risers or along stair treads may be used to provide subtle illumination. Keep stairways clutter-free to minimize the risk of falls.

Treads and Risers

Construct your stairs to make them as easy to use as possible while adhering to local building codes. The *International Residential Code* specifies that stair treads should be at least

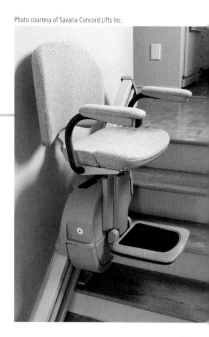

This chairlift's slim design allows people to walk up and down the stairs beside it.

A sturdy railing is essential. Including handrails on both walls would provide even more support.

Photo courtesy of Savaria Concord Lifts Inc.

Residential elevators blend in with custom doors that match the other woodwork in your home. Elevators have become more popular in higher-end homes.

An elevator is a pricier option, but offers a lot of advantages. Some elevators are freestanding; others require a shaft. If you don't need an elevator in your home now, but may want one in the future, make conversion easier by building closets stacked one above another in the same spot on each floor of your home.

Hydraulically powered elevator systems offer quieter operation than stairlifts and provide room for two or more passengers as well as belongings. Some elevators are designed with wood paneling and decorative details and doors that blend with your surrounding living areas. Elevators typically come with an emergency battery system, so they don't get caught between floors during a power outage.

10 inches deep (11 to 12 inches deep is even better) and at least 36 inches wide. Steps with rounded edges (called nosings) and sloping risers no higher than 7¾ inches are the easiest to climb. Steps should all be the same height. If you have open-riser stairs, consider closing the risers for added safety. With long staircases, include a landing each time the staircase changes direction and plan for at least three steps between each landing.

Interior Elevators and Lifts

Consider including a stairlift or elevator in your home or installing an adequate power source near the stairs in case there's a need for a stairlift in the future. With new building or remodeling, you may wish to size interior stairs so a platform lift could be added.

A stairlift is a chair that travels on a track mounted to a load-bearing wall alongside the existing stairs. Seat sizes and motor capacities vary, so you can select the unit that fits your needs. It is also possible to purchase a backup battery pack, which ensures your stairlift will run for a period of time if the power goes out.

Photo courtesy of Savaria Concord Lifts Inc.

Lifts can make entering the house easier when there's not enough space for a ramp. This vertical platform lift allows a person to bypass the stairs.

Cost Estimates

Front Entry Walkway & Lighting

Adding a no-step entry with a roof overhead and a smooth, wide walkway makes life easier—whether you're carrying packages; wheeling a bike, stroller, or luggage; or welcoming a guest who uses a walker or wheelchair. Equally important is the project's appeal as an architectural feature that boosts your home's curb appeal and value. If the existing house front is plain and flat, a new portico can enhance the architecture while providing protection from the elements. Make sure it blends with the home's style and proportions, picking up elements like roof pitch, materials, and trim.

The estimate opposite shows national average costs to build a new 6×12-foot portico entry with two columns and a 48-inch-wide concrete walkway. It also includes new exterior light fixtures: porch ceiling light, three motion-sensor flood lights, lamp post fixture, and low-voltage path lighting. Light fixture costs are for mid-price fixtures available at most home centers.

The estimate includes contractor's labor and overhead. Your project's costs will vary depending on your location, economic conditions, availability of contractors, and the fixtures and materials you select.

Exterior lighting enhances the safety as well as the appearance of your home. Light fixtures should be durable and rated for outdoor use. Use energy-efficient, long-life bulbs, particularly in light fixtures that are difficult to reach, to minimize how often they must be changed.

Estimate Breakdown

Front entry portico including all required demolition for attachment, all rough and finish carpentry, roofing, flashing, and siding. All exposed wood will be primed and painted with two coats of latex paint.	$4,900.00
Electrical work to include a new overhead lighting fixture, a new switch, and all required wiring. Light fixture allowance: $300.00	$900.00
Three-foot-wide by 30-foot-long brick paver walkway including excavation, sand base, and hand-placed brick pavers.	$2,050.00
Demolition debris removal (dumpster)	$600.00

Alternatives:

For broom-finished concrete walkway deduct:	$750.00
For bituminous paving walkway deduct:	$850.00

	Sub-total	**$8,450.00**
	(Add local sales tax for job total)	

Paving Options

Costs per Square Foot Installed

Concrete	$7.25
Concrete pavers	$6.60
Flagstone	$22.25

Other Cost Factors:

- One or more new circuits may need to be added to accommodate outdoor lighting.

- To reduce energy costs, use long-life, energy-efficient, outdoor-approved CFL bulbs that rarely need changing. Choose motion sensor lights that turn on only as needed—or photocell lights that turn on and off automatically at dusk and dawn. Use free-energy solar-powered lights as an add-on to other lighting.

- There could be extra costs for demolition if you have to remove an old walkway, such as concrete that has to be broken up with a jackhammer and hauled away. In some cases, the existing stoop may need to be replaced to support a new portico.

Elevators

As discussed on pages 24–25, universally designed living space is ideally all on one level. If your home has more than one story, you might want to consider having an elevator installed. Costs start at about $16,000 and go up from there if you need to make structural modifications as a retrofit in an existing house. In addition to actual installation costs, you may need the design services of an engineer or architect.

See the estimate for "Exterior Entrance Ramp" on page 143 for related features and costs.

Photo courtesy of Kohler Co.

3

Kitchens

Preparing meals can be a pleasure when a kitchen is designed to accommodate the needs of each household member. The key is to create an attractive space that reduces fatigue or strain. If you minimize the need to bend or reach to place items in the dishwasher, hoist heavy pots of water to the stove, move around obstacles, and clean up messes, you'll have more time to focus on cooking—and enjoying meals with family and friends.

Floor Plan Basics

A universally designed kitchen should have plenty of maneuvering space and access to appliances and storage. The right floor plan will ensure both of these requirements.

Although it's possible to incorporate universal design features into kitchens of almost any size, it is easier to ensure access to work areas if generous square footage is available. Plan for wide doorways between the kitchen and adjoining rooms; if doors are included, make certain they do not interfere with access to appliances or storage.

Whether you plan on having two cooks working together or want to provide access for a cook who uses a wheelchair, allot a minimum of 30×48 inches of clear space in front of each appliance or work area and include 42- to 48-inch-wide aisles for easy movement. A 5-foot circle of open floor space provides turning room for wheelchair

users—plus it allows for multiple cooks and/or entertaining in the kitchen area.

Kitchen Layouts

The kitchen work triangle (which effectively positions the refrigerator, sink, and cooktop or range at the points) has long been a staple of kitchen design because it makes it easy to move between work centers. But don't feel constrained by the work triangle—the key is to find the best kitchen layout that works for you and anyone else who may use the kitchen. Consider the common kitchen layouts below and how you might be able to use or modify each to fit your requirements and available space.

One-wall kitchens place all of the appliances and cabinets along a single wall. This layout may not be the most efficient, but it saves space in a small kitchen and allows the cook to move items from one workstation to the next with minimal effort. If you have the space, plan for at least 4 feet of counter between appliances.

Galley layouts, which are built between two parallel walls, also allow a cook to move easily between work areas. With 5 feet of open floor space between cabinets, more than one cook or people who use wheelchairs should have room

Photo courtesy of General Electric Company

This kitchen's compact work triangle still provides plenty of room to move. Elevated appliances reduce the need for bending and provide access for seated users.

A spacious, L-shaped kitchen with an island provides plenty of easy-to-reach storage and workspace for multiple cooks—just make sure aisles are wide enough for easy movement. An eat-in kitchen minimizes the distance required to carry food or dishes.

to work. But spacing the walls too far apart may make it difficult for a cook to reach items without wasting steps.

L-shaped kitchens should concentrate the work centers near the crook of the L, allowing cooks to move items with minimal lifting and minimize the movement required between workstations.

U-shaped layouts connect work areas located on three walls. Including an island with a sink, cooktop, or extra prep area can make a U-shaped kitchen more efficient. It's best to allow at least 5 feet of open workspace in the center so there's plenty of room to work.

Compact workstations and open leg room make this specialized L-shaped kitchen functional. A bonus: the entire adjustable-height work area can be raised or lowered with the push of a button.

A narrow galley-style kitchen minimizes movement between work areas but may make it crowded for more than one cook to work. This island appears to be floating because of an unusual recessed base and angled cabinets. Removable drawers and drawer glides would provide even more leg room for seated cooks.

Work Centers

The main kitchen work centers involve food prep, cooking, and cleanup, so allow plenty of room for each. If you have the space, consider specialty areas, such as a baking center or desk.

Food preparation, cooking, and cleanup overlap throughout the kitchen, but each involves slightly different tasks and considerations.

Food Prep

A section of continuous countertop at least 36 inches wide, preferably with open knee space beneath, is ideal for food preparation for seated cooks. Varied countertop heights allow people of different statures to work together and make it possible for people to sit while undertaking some tasks and stand for others.

The more GFCI electrical outlets, the better, as this makes it easy to plug in small appliances wherever you would like to use them. If possible, plan the refrigerator and other food storage close to the food prep area so items are easy to reach.

Cooking

The most important cooking components are the cooktop or range and microwave oven. Wall ovens may be placed outside the main task area, although for ease of use, it helps to have them nearby. The cooktop or range should also include an overhead ventilation hood or a downdraft vent. Include at least 12 inches of heat-resistant countertop on one side of the cooktop and at least 15 inches on the other as landing space for hot pots. Plan for another area at least 15 inches above, below, or adjacent to the microwave and wall oven. Also include easy-to-reach storage for cooking tools, such as pots and pans, utensils, potholders, and spices. A pot-filler faucet within close reach of the

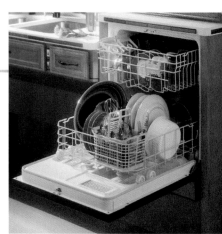

Elevating a dishwasher reduces bending and improves access to the cleanup zone. Place the dishwasher within 3 feet of the sink to make loading easier.

Photo courtesy of General Electric Company

cooktop or range eliminates the need to carry large, heavy pots of water to the stove.

Cleanup

Because the sink is used for so many tasks, it is often located at the center of the work triangle. A garbage disposal is helpful for cleanup, but it can get in the way of open knee space under the sink; should you choose to include one, you may wish to position it beneath one bowl of a double sink so there's still leg room under the other bowl for seated users. The dishwasher should ideally be located to one side of the sink. Include at least one waste receptacle nearby; you may wish to plan space for a compost or recycling center as well. Storage is important here, too: storing everyday dishes, glassware, and utensils adjacent to the dishwasher makes for easy unloading, and stashing dish towels and cleaning products within reach ensures they're easy to grab when needed.

Photo courtesy of Kohler Co.

Food prep, cooking, and cleanup can all be done in one spot with this sink cook center. Once you're finished with your water-based cooking, the water drains from the pot into the sink with the push of a button.

Photo courtesy of General Electric

A rolling cart that moves easily around the kitchen serves as a portable workstation for food prep, serving, or cleanup. When not in use, it tucks beneath the open knee space otherwise reserved for seated cooks.

Specialty Work Centers

If you have the opportunity to customize the elements you include in your newly built or remodeled kitchen, consider including specialty work centers for added convenience. A busy family with small children might appreciate a snack zone located outside the work triangle that includes a refrigerator drawer stocked with beverages and easy-to-reach drawers filled with munchies. If someone in your family loves to bake, consider a baking area with a countertop lowered to 30 inches high rather than the standard 36 inches; this allows the cook to sit while kneading dough or frosting cupcakes to avoid fatigue or back strain. A desk area for meal-planning, homework, bill paying, and organization keeps clutter out of the work triangle and minimizes trips between rooms.

By the Numbers

Here are a few specific universal design recommendations that should help you plan the location of work centers, courtesy of the National Kitchen and Bath Association. You will find additional recommendations throughout this chapter.

- In a kitchen with three work centers (food prep, cooking, and cleanup), the sum of the traveled distances between the legs of the work triangle should be no more than 26 feet.

- A single leg of the work triangle should measure no less than 4 feet or more than 9 feet.

- Keep major traffic flow out of the basic work triangle.

- If the kitchen has only one sink, locate it adjacent to or across from the cooking surface and refrigerator.

- Include at least 3 feet of countertop in the food prep work area, preferably with knee space underneath.

- Create staging or landing areas with at least 15 inches of countertop no more than 48 inches away from all major appliances, including the refrigerator, microwave, and wall oven.

Countertops

In a universally designed kitchen, countertop materials should be durable and easy to clean. Carefully planning countertop layout ensures it will meet your needs for the long-term.

If possible, include at least two countertop heights in your kitchen: 36 to 45 inches for a standard work surface (depending on the height of the primary user), and 28 to 32 inches to allow people of all heights—including children or seated users—to work together in the kitchen. Ideally, at least part of the kitchen should include open knee space—36 inches wide and 27 inches high—under the counter as well.

Placement

Install countertops that are at least 24 inches deep on both sides of the sink, refrigerator, and cooktop or range to provide a safe landing spot for everything from hot pans to groceries. An expanse of smooth, scratch-resistant countertop between workstations allows you to slide heavy pots across the surface rather than carry them.

Laminate is a durable, reasonably priced countertop option. Dark countertops provide strong visual contrast with wood cabinets and light-color walls.

The contrast of the light-color edging, sink, and faucet against this dark island countertop makes them easy to spot, particularly for people with limited vision.

Materials

In choosing your countertop material, consider the following:

Laminate. Perhaps the most affordably priced and widely used countertop surface, laminate is made from layers of plastic sheeting and particleboard bound together under heat and pressure. Laminate is durable, easy to clean, and available in a variety of colors and designs—some styles imitate wood, stone, and ceramic tile. It may scratch and wear thin over time, however, and is not heat-resistant.

Photo courtesy of Wilsonart Laminate

Photo courtesy of Wilsonart Solid Surface

Specialized adjustable-height countertops/cabinets have an electronic mechanism that allows you to move them up and down to the desired height (far left).

This solid-surface countertop features a custom drainboard and seamless design so it's easy to clean (left). Some solid-surface brands are resistant to stains, mold, and mildew.

Stone. Available in tile or slab form, stone is generally durable. Slabs will cost more than tile but don't require grouting or grout care. Although it is expensive, granite is one of the best options because it is easy to maintain, elegant, and virtually indestructible (although in rare cases it may scratch). Limestone, slate, marble, and soapstone are other options, although they may be prone to stains and wear.

Quartz Composite. Made of crushed quartz blended with color pigments and plastic resins, this hard, dense material requires no sealing and can be used on countertops, backsplashes, and walls. It resists scratching and heat and is easy to clean and maintain. It does not look as natural as real stone, however.

Solid surface. These countertops require minimal maintenance and are more durable than laminate because they are cast from acrylic resin. Intense heat and heavy falling objects may damage the surface, but minor scratches and abrasions can be repaired. Rounded edge treatments make the countertops safer; inlaid designs ensure edges are visible.

Ceramic tile. Clay-based ceramic tiles are available in a variety of colors, patterns, shapes, and sizes. The tiles are durable and easy to care for, but the grout may be hard to clean.

Other kitchen countertop materials include stainless steel, hardwoods, butcher block, concrete, and sustainable surfacing made from recycled materials, such as glass.

Additional Features

Raised-edge details may prevent spills and help people with limited eyesight better see the edge of the countertop (particularly if the edge is a contrasting color). Preparing light-colored foods on dark countertops (and vice versa) is easier, so consider combining light and dark surfaces in food prep areas by using a different countertop material on the island. Include special features for more convenience, such as cutouts that help people with limited strength hold mixing bowls in place or routed drain boards that are built into solid surfacing so water runs into the sink rather than all over the countertop.

Easy-Clean Options

Because of the myriad items that rest on surfaces in the kitchen—from raw meats to fresh veggies—keeping countertops clean is particularly important. In general, the smoother the surface of the countertop, the easier it is to clean. Less porous materials, such as solid surfacing, are also a good choice because they don't stain as easily. An antibacterial synthetic countertop reduces germs, which helps with cleaning. Natural quartz is available with built-in antimicrobial protection to fight the growth of odor-causing bacteria, mold, and mildew.

Sinks & Faucets

Kitchen sinks must withstand a lot of use, so select a high-quality, durable basin and faucet. If there's room, you may wish to include a smaller secondary sink in the food prep area as well.

Standing at the sink—whether you're rinsing vegetables or washing dishes—can cause strain on your back and knees, particularly if the sink isn't positioned at the right height. Ideally, the sink rim should be no more than 34 inches high. For ultimate flexibility (and so family members of all heights and abilities can help with the dishes), you might consider an adjustable-height sink that raises or lowers to between 29 and 40 inches with the push of a button.

Offset drains help free up storage or knee space beneath the sink—particularly important for seated users. Plan for a minimum of 36 inches wide by 27 inches high by 8 inches deep, increasing to 17 inches deep in the toe space. Cabinet doors that fold out of the way or are removable can be installed to hide knee access when it's not in use. To protect against burns, insulate sink pipes or install a removable panel to cover them.

one side of the sink and at least 18 inches wide on the other so there's room to place dishes and groceries. In addition to the main sink, you may wish to add a second, smaller prep sink in an island or along a stretch of countertop for use by a second cook.

If you move the sink or dishwasher to a new wall when remodeling, there will be greater expense for rough-in plumbing.

Sink Configurations

Regardless of the sink configuration, keep in mind that shallower sinks are easier to use. Universal design guidelines recommend that a sink bowl be no more than 6½ inches deep; deeper bowls require more bending. If you prefer a deeper bowl for stacking dirty dishes or soaking big pans, look for a sink that includes one deep bowl and one shallow one or a smaller bowl inset between two larger ones.

Sink Placement

Locating the sink between the stove and refrigerator is easiest for food preparation. Include at least a 24-inch-wide landing area to

A pot-filler faucet installed on the wall behind the cooktop or range allows cooks to fill pots right where they use them, rather than hauling heavy pots from sink to stove.

Photo courtesy of GROHE America, Inc.

Photo courtesy of Kohler Co.

Photo courtesy of Moen Incorporated

A one-handle faucet with a pull-out spout is easy to operate and attractive.

Sink Materials

Today's sinks are manufactured from a variety of materials to fit your needs and tastes. The most common include:

Stainless steel. These sinks are available at modest prices, are easy to install, and come in a variety of finishes. Look for thick walls and a high percentage of nickel and chromium so they don't scratch as easily.

Porcelain-enamel cast iron. Sinks made of this heavy material hold water temperatures longer than others and are durable, although hard porcelain surfaces can chip and scratch.

Composite. Minerals such as quartz or granite are mixed with an acrylic- or polyester-resin base to create these sinks. Composite sinks may be expensive, but they're durable and easy to care for.

Fireclay. This dense, durable, low-maintenance material is often used to create country-style sinks and may feature painted designs.

Solid surface. Like solid-surface countertops, these sinks are easy to care for and resist scratches and chips. Solid surfacing is available in many colors and patterns; sinks are integrated with countertops of the same material for a seamless setup.

A second sink can be helpful in a food prep area. This stainless-steel, undermount version matches the style of the main kitchen sink nearby.

Kitchen Faucets

When you select a faucet, make sure the faucet height and sink depth are compatible to avoid splashes. The most functional models are tall enough to fill pots, with pull-outs to rinse all corners of the sink. Beyond these basic considerations, take into account:

- **Style.** A single-lever faucet is easiest to use, whether your hands are messy or you have limited hand strength. A faucet that includes a pull-out sprayer makes it easier to rinse the sink or fill pots without lifting them.

- **Finish.** Polished finishes stand out; brushed finishes are more subdued. Chrome is popular because it holds up well and doesn't require protective coatings. Other finishes include brass, nickel, pewter, bronze, and gold.

- **Placement.** Placing the faucet at the side of the sink rather than the back makes it easier to reach the controls.

- **Safety.** Look for a faucet with a scald-guard valve, which protects against sudden changes in water temperature.

- **Convenience.** Hands-free faucets may be activated by motion sensors or a foot pedal. Hot water dispensers installed next to the regular faucet allow you to make hot tea or other drinks without turning on the stove.

Easy-Clean Options

When it comes to cooking cleanup, the sink often draws the biggest messes. Self-rimming sinks have a lip sealed with caulk, which tends to collect dirt, mildew, and soap scum. Undermount models make it easier to wipe messes from the counter into the sink. Better yet, opt for an integral sink. The bowl and surrounding countertop are made from a large piece of the same material, so there aren't any seams to collect dirt.

Appliances

Appliances are the focal points of most kitchen activities. With a smart combination of universal and pro-style features, culinary masterpieces are within almost everyone's reach (cooking skills notwithstanding).

Although individual kitchen appliances look and function differently, some considerations apply across the board. If you are purchasing new appliances, look for ENERGY STAR-qualified models, which provide considerable energy savings. Because loud exhaust fans or dishwashers can make it hard for people to hear conversations, try to purchase the quietest models available. And make certain buttons and labels on appliances are easy to read—the larger the type, the better.

Of course, ergonomics are important, too. Dials at least 1½ inches in diameter with click stops indicating which setting has been selected and a handle shape that does not require twisting or grasping are easiest to operate. Controls located at the front or side of appliances are safer and easier to reach than those situated at the back (unless you have small children in the house). Pull-out shelves and racks make it easier to use any appliance. Most universal design guidelines recommend at least 15 inches of countertop

Electric cooktops are easy to operate and clean. It's best to select models with burner indicators so people with limited vision can see where the burners begin.

Photo courtesy of General Electric Company

Photo courtesy of General Electric Company

An open stretch of heat-proof countertop adjacent to a wall oven ensures there's a place to put hot dishes.

landing space above, below, or to each side of an appliance.

Ranges, Cooktops, and Ovens

Kitchens include either an all-in-one range or a separate cooktop and wall oven. Regardless of which option you choose, plan for countertop landing space on either side of each cooking appliance. In addition, cooktops should have a correctly sized, ducted ventilation system (at least 150 cfm) with controls that are easy to reach.

A range isn't as easy to use as a separate cooktop and wall oven because it's necessary to bend over to place heavy pans in the oven. If you opt for a range, select a self-cleaning model that has controls located on the front or side of the appliance. If possible, provide knee space next to the range to make it easier for seated cooks to place items in the oven.

Because cooktops can be installed at any height, they are great for universally designed kitchens. Lowering the cooktop to 34 inches and creating knee space beneath is optimal for seated cooks. For most people, electric cooktops with burners beneath a smooth, solid surface are easier to use than electric coil or gas versions because you can slide pots and pans from the countertop

to the cooktop. For safety, select models with staggered burners to eliminate reaching over hot burners, and make certain the cooktop has a heat indicator light or burners that glow so you know when parts of the appliance are still hot. If you opt for an overhead ventilation hood, look for one with a wireless remote control so you don't have to reach up to turn the fan on or off. Or consider a cooktop with a downdraft venting system, with vents at the center and back equipped with high-power fans to pull hot air away from the cook.

Wall ovens can be mounted at heights efficient for standing or seated cooks. Ideally, one oven rack should be located at countertop height and the oven controls should be positioned no higher than 48 inches above the floor. Include a stretch of countertop adjacent to the oven for transferring dishes. A door that swings open to the side rather than down allows you to get closer to the oven without leaning across the hot door. With a side-swing oven door, you can include a pull-out counter beneath the oven. Choose an oven with good interior lighting so you needn't open the oven door as often.

Refrigerators and Freezers

A side-by-side unit that places the freezer on one side and the refrigerator on the other is one of the best options for users of a variety of heights, sizes, and abilities. Shelves at different heights allow children, seated users, and standing adults to access different portions of the refrigerator. Counter-depth units make it easier to reach or see what's in the back of the fridge. Another option is a side-by-side refrigerator with a freezer drawer on the bottom

Raising the height of the dishwasher minimizes back strain caused by bending over to load dishes. For further convenience, leave enough floor space next to the dishwasher so you can sit while tackling a large load.

or a drawer-style refrigerator. (See the sidebar on the next page.)

Dishwashers

The dishwasher should be located within 36 inches of the nearest edge of a cleanup or food prep sink. Raising the dishwasher 6 to 12 inches off the floor minimizes the amount of bending required to load and unload dishes. Provide at least 21 inches of standing space between the edge of the dishwasher and any countertop or cabinets placed at a right angle to it.

A number of features make today's dishwashers particularly user-friendly. Look for racks that

Regardless of the configuration, certain features—including spill-proof shelves that slide out, see-through bins, and an ice and water dispenser in the door—make any refrigerator and freezer easier to use.

A pull-out landing area provides a spot for setting hot dishes below the microwave. No matter where the microwave oven is placed, try to allow for at least 15 inches of clear surface above, below, or adjacent to it.

slide in and out smoothly as well as flexible loading features such as fold-down tines. An easy-to-read display with push buttons rather than a large knob is better, particularly for people with small hands or arthritis. A lock switch or lever that protects against accidental operation is a good idea, too.

Microwave Ovens

In many homes, microwave ovens are placed too high, which makes them hard to reach and even dangerous. Instead, place your microwave oven on the countertop or mount it on the wall at a height that's convenient for your home's users. For optimal access when standing, place the bottom of the microwave 3 inches below the primary user's shoulder or no higher than 54 inches above the floor. If shorter people and seated users need to reach the microwave oven, place it with the controls less than 48 inches from the floor, but at least 15 inches off the finished floor.

Specialty Drawers

Want an alternative to your standard refrigerator, dishwasher, or oven? Consider the convenience of specialty drawers, which save floor space and require minimal reaching and bending when positioned at the right height. With cabinetry-matching panels, you can even disguise your specialty drawers.

- **Refrigerator or freezer drawers** are designed to fit into existing cabinetry. Two drawers stacked inside the work triangle may be all the chilled storage needed in a small kitchen. Or position a drawer near the microwave oven to create a snack zone outside the main work triangle.

- **Dishwasher drawers** make cleanup easy. Place heavy-duty items in one and more delicate glassware in the other; or just run one drawer at a time so you always have clean dishes on hand.

- **Warming drawers** are ideal whether you have a large family or like to entertain. They're designed to prevent moist foods from drying out and maintain crispness of other foods. Use one to keep side dishes at serving temperature until the main course is prepared or to keep leftovers warm until family members arrive home for dinner.

Flooring

Water and other spills, dropped objects, and heavy traffic can wreak havoc on kitchen flooring. Your best bet is an attractive, durable surface that is easy to clean and comfortable underfoot.

When you're working in a space surrounded by hard surfaces (such as the kitchen), a nonslip floor material becomes even more important for safety. Look for flooring with a matte finish, which is less likely to be slippery or create glare. Because most work in the kitchen requires you to be on your feet, you also may want to consider a cushioned material to reduce back strain and leg fatigue.

The COF (or coefficient of friction) is the measure of how slip-resistant a surface is. Make certain the flooring in your kitchen has a COF of at least 0.6. Two top choices are solid vinyl with a matte surface and cork.

Flooring Materials

An inexpensive, easy-to-maintain material that is relatively comfortable to stand on, solid vinyl is a popular choice for kitchens. It

Patterned cork tiles create a playful kitchen floor. Cork is valued for its resilience, comfort, and sustainability as a recommended "green" flooring material. Cork flooring is also moisture-resistant, ideal for the kitchen.

Sheet vinyl is a common kitchen flooring material available in a variety of colors and patterns. Here, no thresholds are necessary because the same flooring continues in the adjacent seating area.

Durable, stain- and moisture-resistant ceramic tiles work well in kitchens as long as they have a nonslip, matte, or textured finish. Opt for neutral-color tiles to reduce eyestrain.

Changes Underfoot

Flooring surfaces and levels often change between rooms or even within a room, which can be a tripping hazard. Using the same flooring material throughout the home and removing any thresholds between rooms is perhaps the safest option. But many homeowners opt for harder surfaces such as nonslip ceramic tile or vinyl in kitchens, bathrooms, and entries and softer materials, such as low-pile carpet, in living spaces. To minimize these flooring changes, square thresholds should be offset by no more than ¼ inch and slanted thresholds by no more than ½ inch. Within a room, adding a border of contrasting flooring around the perimeter marks boundaries, which helps people with limited vision.

Hardwood is a beautiful flooring option, but it may be more slippery than other materials. Learn more about hardwood options on page 22.

is available in two styles: Rotogravure vinyl features a knobby texture and has color and pattern printed on the finished side, while inlaid vinyl has color and pattern that runs through the thickness of the material for improved durability. Vinyl is available in various tile sizes (with either a dry back laid in adhesive or a peel-and-stick backing) or in 6- and 12-foot-wide sheets. The benefit of vinyl tile is that you can replace individual damaged tiles rather than the whole floor; the drawback is that the seams between the tiles may trap dirt. Sheet vinyl, on the other hand, has few seams, so cleaning is relatively easy.

Cork flooring is a great option that is warm, comfortable, and noiseless. This moisture- and temperature-resistant material usually comes in 12×12-inch tiles made from the renewable bark of cork oak trees. It has a grain similar to that of burled hardwood and is available in a variety of stains. Plus cleaning is easy: simply sweep and mop the floor for regular maintenance.

Walls & Color

Color sets the mood, defines a room's details, and can even affect appetites. One of the easiest ways to add impact to the kitchen is by adding color on the floor, cabinets, and especially the walls.

In the kitchen, color pulls double duty. It adds serious style to a space where your family probably spends a lot of time. But it also helps people with reduced vision see parts of the room in relation to one another, which is key for kitchen safety. For instance, a colorful countertop that contrasts with white appliances ensures the cooktop and other items are easier to see.

Designing the kitchen with high contrast ensures that items are easily visible, but it also allows you to have fun with color. Painting the walls a bright hue adds energy to a kitchen even as it ensures that white light switches, window frames, and baseboards stand out.

On the Walls

Backsplashes are a common wall treatment in kitchens, valued as much for their style as for the way they protect the wall from messes. A backsplash may be the same material as the countertop, or it may be a different material as an accent. Wall tiles are less durable than floor or countertop tiles; feel free to use hardier

Photo courtesy of Armstrong World Industries, Inc.

The color of these walls contrasts with the natural hue of the flooring and the light wood cabinetry. A short backsplash protects the walls right above the countertops.

countertop tiles on the wall, but avoid using delicate wall tiles on the countertop. Consider a backsplash of handmade or sculptural tiles, which often are too expensive to use in large quantities. Watch out for glare, however. Rather than installing an entire backsplash of iridescent tile, use a single row or two to break up an expanse of matte-finish tiles.

Beyond decorative backsplashes, keep kitchen wall treatments simple. Paint is easiest to apply and provides endless color options. Satin- or eggshell-finish latex paint allows you to wipe up cooking splatters more easily than flat paint does. Vinyl wallpaper is another smart choice because it resists stains and is easy to remove if sizing is applied underneath. Select a textured paper to reduce glare.

Neutral-color walls and large windows provide a subtle backdrop for dramatic lime-green cabinetry. The bright cabinet hue makes it easy to spot the stainless-steel appliances and dark countertops.

Photo © Andersen Corporation

A quality kitchen lighting scheme is attractive as well as functional. Include a combination of windows and task and ambient lighting in your illumination plan to ensure you can see what you're doing.

Lighting & Windows

Lighting for Aging

People of different ages have different lighting needs. "Most people are not aware of the changes that our eyes go through as we age," says Eunice Noell-Waggoner, L.C., President of the Center of Design for an Aging Society. "Older people need higher levels of light without glare." Smart lighting will make your kitchen friendly for all ages. Consider these tips:

- **Choose the right fixture.** Aging eyes take on a yellow filter, so select bulbs that balance out yellow tones. With their bluish cast, full-spectrum bulbs are a good option. "I promote fluorescents—you can buy them with good color," Noell-Waggoner says. Low-voltage halogen bulbs also work well.

- **Light indirectly.** "Bounce light off the ceiling, upper walls, and cabinets," Noell-Waggoner recommends. "You want to block the brightness of the light source that would be glare-producing."

- **Take surfaces into account.** Surfaces may cause glare. "Light reflects off a polished surface and bounces up into your eyes," Noell-Waggoner says. "Choose a matte finish for countertops."

- **Include night lighting.** Dim halogen rope lights above cabinets create night lighting.

Upon entering the kitchen, you should be able to see exactly where you're going and what you're doing with the flip of a switch. Install rocker switches 44 to 48 inches above the floor for easy access. Another option is motion-detector lighting, which turns on when you enter the room and off when you leave.

Windows

There's nothing like natural light to enhance your mood. Energy-efficient, operable windows and skylights should cover an area equal to at least 10 percent of the total square footage of the kitchen. Reduce the number of upper cabinets along exterior walls to provide more window space. Skylights usher in diffuse daylight without taking up wall space. Install blinds or other treatments to filter light and provide privacy.

Lighting

Kitchen lighting is most efficient when it's from multiple sources. In addition to general overhead lighting from ceiling-mount fixtures, track lights, or recessed cans, include task lighting with separate controls at work surfaces. To minimize shadows on countertops, install undercabinet lighting. Pendants perform a similar function over an island. In-cabinet lights illuminate the contents of glass-door cabinets. Ambient lighting mounted above upper cabinets produces a rich glow.

Photo courtesy of Progress Lighting

The LED light fixtures used to illuminate this kitchen—including mini-pendants and recessed fixtures—are energy efficient, produce a warm white light, and emit little heat.

Storage Solutions

Glide-out, pull-down, pop-up. You name it, and today's kitchen cabinetry probably does it, making storage of and access to pots, cooking utensils, and food items easier than ever.

Reaching is easiest between the waist and the shoulders, so it makes sense to store the majority of items at that height. The problem is most kitchen storage is located in base cabinets close to the floor or wall cabinets above the work area—which may mean frequent bending or reaching to grab items. What's the solution? An artful mix of open and closed storage positioned at a variety of heights.

Storage Basics

Plan storage of frequently used items 15 inches to 48 inches above the floor so people who are seated can reach them with minimal effort. In lower cabinets, items stored in drawers or on roll-out shelves are easier to see and reach; if lower shelves don't roll out, it helps if they are no more than 10 inches deep. Include a lazy Susan to take advantage of available space in corner cabinets. Upper cabinets needn't reach the ceiling—few people can grab what's stored on the top shelves. Specialized height-adjustable cabinets that electronically or hydraulically move up and down the wall put items you need within reach.

Store heavier, larger items such as pots, pans, and platters in lower cabinets or large drawers; lighter items such as cereal bowls and drinking glasses can be stored above the countertop, as long as the shelves aren't too high. Primary food storage is best placed near the longest stretch of countertop so you can grab items while cooking; situate food items that are used less often in cabinets outside the work triangle or in a pantry.

You may wish to use other storage options to supplement standard cabinetry. Rolling carts with shelves or drawers allow you to move frequently used items around the kitchen as needed. Hang items such as cooking utensils on the wall near the cooktop so they're easy to grab. Appliance garages with tambour doors allow you to stash small appliances such as toasters on the countertop without cluttering your work surface. And remember the

A roll-out tray divider organizes cutting boards and cookie trays.

Photo courtesy of KraftMaid Cabinetry

Photo courtesy of KraftMaid Cabinetry

The cutting board, cutlery divider, and miscellaneous drawers keep daily cooking utensils and dishware well-organized and within easy reach.

Customizing Cabinetry

Cabinets are available in stock, semi-custom, and custom models. Many stock and semi-custom options offer possibilities for customization. Working with a cabinetmaker to design custom cabinets ensures the size, shape, and configuration of your kitchen cabinetry exactly fits your needs and lifestyle. If customized cabinets are out of your price range, consider these modifications for stock or semi-custom cabinets:

- **Upper cabinets.** Install cabinet doors with glass-front panels so you can see where items are stored to minimize the time and energy spent searching. Better yet, remove cabinet doors to make accessing items easier, or purchase less expensive open shelving instead.

- **Base cabinets.** If possible, consider cabinet doors that slide back into the cabinet base rather than those that open outward. Purchase removable base cabinets that can be used as storage now, but may be taken out later to create open knee space.

convenience of large, easy-access containers for baking ingredients, tea bags, and other items.

Hardware

Selecting the right hardware improves access to the contents of cabinets and drawers. Pulls are easier to grasp than knobs; in particular, C-shaped or D-shaped handles that are large enough for you to slip your fingers through work best. Or try cabinets with magnetic latches, which allow you to push on the outside of the door to pop it open. In addition, test drawers to make sure they slide in and out smoothly. Full-extension hardware helps drawers pull out farther than normal, making it easier to access items in the back of the drawer.

This pull-out base cabinet allows you to see and access items stored in the back.

Photo courtesy of KraftMaid Cabinetry

Deep drawers allow you to store pots, pans, and other cooking essentials close to countertop height to minimize bending.

Photo courtesy of KraftMaid Cabinetry

Photo courtesy of KraftMaid Cabinetry

Photo courtesy of KraftMaid Cabinetry

Pop-up shelves keep heavy mixers and other appliances out of the way but easy to access. This version includes an easy-click lever that lifts your mixer to a custom height.

If there isn't room for a large pantry in your kitchen, consider a pull-out pantry unit for storing bottles, cans, and dry goods right where you use them most.

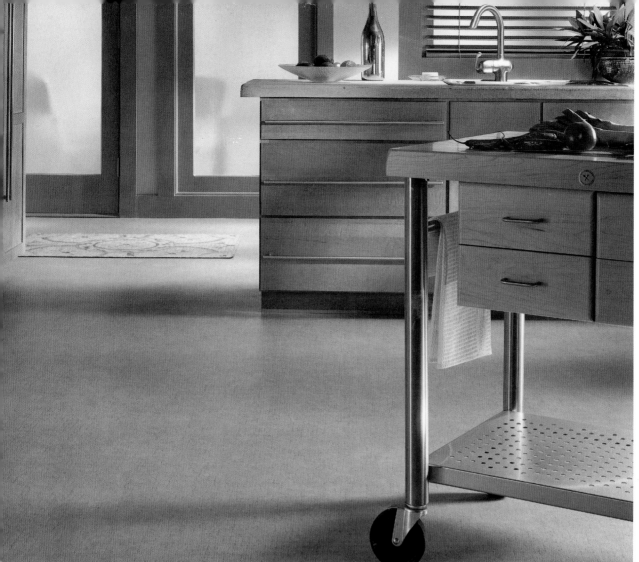

Rolling carts outfitted with drawers provide storage and work space that can be used anywhere in the kitchen.

Two carousels in this corner base unit take advantage of space that otherwise would be out of reach.

This shelving lowers as needed to allow access to dishware and other kitchen necessities.

Kitchens *49*

Cost Estimates
Kitchen Remodeling

Adding universal design elements can run the gamut from a simple replacement of drawer and cabinet hardware all the way to a complete remodel. If you're ready to invest in a kitchen update, it's a great opportunity to make the space more accessible for current and future comfort, ease of use, and enjoyment.

This estimate covers the costs to completely gut and remodel a basic, single-wall kitchen, incorporating universal design features to make it accessible to a seated user. The work includes removing all elements of the old kitchen, down to the studs, then installing new drywall, cabinets and solid surface (e.g., Corian® or Surell®) countertops, nonslip tile flooring, appliances, a sink and faucet, light fixtures and outlets, plus trim and painting.

The materials are mostly mid-price range, including stock cabinets, fixtures, and appliances available in home centers. Your choices for these items will substantially affect project costs. Contractor's labor and overhead are included in the estimate, based on national averages, and will vary depending on your location, availability of contractors and materials, and economic conditions. See the boxes at left for costs for other flooring and countertop options, per square or linear foot, installed.

A complete kitchen update provides the opportunity to create a stylish, functional room such as this one. Ample work surfaces, wide aisles, and convenient storage make this kitchen easy to use and attractive.

Countertop Materials

Costs per Linear Foot Installed	
Plastic laminate	$55.50
Ceramic tile	$58.00
Stone	$157.00
Solid surface	$126.00
Engineered stone	$82.00

Flooring Options

Costs per Square Foot Installed	
Pre-finished oak strip	$10.70
Floating laminate	$9.00
Sheet vinyl	$8.25
Vinyl tiles	$6.05

Photo © Jupiterimages

Estimate Breakdown

Basic, single-wall kitchen remodel to include all required demolition and disconnections and installation of framing and blocking, insulation, drywall, ceramic tile floor, cabinets, and solid surface countertop.	$14,000.00
Cabinetry allowance: $3,500.00 Countertop allowance: $1,000.00 Appliance allowance: $3,200.00	
Plumbing to include installation of new kitchen sink and dishwasher.	$850.00
Electrical work to include all rough wiring, outlets, switches and fixtures as per plan.	$900.00
Demolition debris removal (dumpster)	$875.00
Sub-total	**$16,625.00**
(Add local sales tax for job total)	

Photo © Jupiterimages

Task lighting is critical in the kitchen to adequately illuminate work surfaces and eliminate shadows. Position fixtures such as these contemporary-look pendant lights above a kitchen island.

Return on Investment

Renovating a kitchen or bath tops the list for projects that pay you back when you sell your home. A partial remodel tends to bring more value per dollar spent than a full-blown, luxury renovation. Key to added value are how dated the old kitchen is, how well the new work blends with your home's architecture, and attention to trends such as ample counter space, dual sinks, cooktops, stainless appliances, and a pantry or eating area. Neutral colors are best if you're thinking about resale. Crown molding is a popular feature that builders use throughout homes to enhance sales appeal at relatively low cost.

Universal design features should strengthen your kitchen's value by making it useful to a broader range of people, provided the features that add comfort and ease of use are well blended into the decor.

Photo courtesy of Kohler Co.

4

Bathrooms

Once valued solely for their functionality, bathrooms now double as spa-like retreats in many homes. They're the perfect private havens for indulging in the luxury of a long soak in the tub or an energizing shower. Yet navigating a bathroom with its variety of hard fixtures and slippery surfaces raises safety concerns. Fortunately, innovative products and ideas make it easier to design a bathroom that's safe, user-friendly, and beautiful, too.

Floor Plan Basics

When it comes to designing a comfortable bathroom, bigger is more luxurious, but universal bathrooms can be achieved in moderately sized spaces as well. Additional square footage allows for widened doorways and ample clearance room.

Most bathrooms are designed around three primary elements: the sink, toilet, and a bathing fixture (a shower, tub, or both). When building or remodeling a bath, consider the best location for fixtures based on available space and the most cost-effective plumbing installation. It may make sense to locate the sink, toilet, and shower on one wall to minimize the amount of rough-in plumbing work. Spreading these fixtures out on two or three walls will improve traffic patterns within the room but may substantially increase installation costs. Planning the layout with care makes the bath more usable, without having to concern yourself with costly—and disruptive—future modifications.

Throughout this chapter, you will find specific recommendations to ensure that each functional area of the bathroom has ample approach space and clearance room for wheelchair or walker use. Even if you never need this type of clearance, the open floor space will contribute to a luxurious finished bath. In general, plan for at least a 5-foot circle of open floor space for wheelchair maneuverability between bathroom fixtures. Passages between bathroom walls and fixtures should be at least 36 inches wide. A minimum approach area of 30×48 inches is recommended in front of the sink and 36×60 inches in front of the tub; the toilet should be located in the corner of a 60×60-inch square. The clearances for these fixtures may overlap, as long as the space between two areas meets the minimum guidelines for both.

Photo courtesy of Moen Incorporated

Adding safety bars that attach directly to the tub side or toilet seat is an inexpensive, effective way to make a bathroom more accessible. Tubs with flat floors are best suited for freestanding stools like this one.

A master bedroom that flows into the bath with the same flooring can help eliminate barriers, such as thresholds and doors.

At the Door

Doorways that are 34 to 36 inches wide allow for easy entrance to the bathroom. Swing-clear hinges can help avoid costly door widening in remodeling by effectively adding 1½ to 2 inches of clear opening width. Standard doors may require up to 10 square feet of floor space to swing open; consider installing pocket doors to reserve that floor space for other uses. If you do stick with traditional doors, you may wish to install one that opens toward the hall rather than into the bathroom. That way, if someone falls near the door, you'll be able to get in and help. Make sure the hallway outside the door is wide enough so the open door won't block passage.

Form and Function

Bathrooms take a variety of forms and uses, from spacious master baths to powder rooms. It may be impossible to fit all of the universal design recommendations laid out in this chapter in every bath in your house. Ideally, at least one main-floor bath should be as spacious and easy to access as possible.

The additional floor space in a roomy master bath allows you to include furnishings, such as a comfortable (and sturdy) chair for sitting while drying off or dressing. Later, the furnishings can be removed if wheelchair access space is needed.

Grab Bars

Grab bars are key for ensuring safety in the bathroom by helping people steady themselves when getting in and out of the tub or up and down from the toilet. Grab bars should meet the following guidelines:

- They should withstand a 250-pound load, which means they must be installed into the wall studs or a wall that is reinforced. To reinforce a wall, install blocking or affix ¾-inch plywood backing to the wall framing. Even if you don't plan to install grab bars in your home now, building the proper reinforcement into the wall during construction makes it easier to add them later.

- Grab bars should be 1¼ to 2 inches in diameter to fit comfortably between the thumb and fingers and should project 1½ inches from the wall for easy grasping.

- Horizontal grab bars should be installed 33 to 36 inches above the floor behind and to at least one side of the toilet.

- In the shower, horizontal grab bars should be installed on both shower walls 32 to 48 inches from the floor.

- A vertical bar may be installed at the entrance to the tub; the bottom of the bar should be 32 to 38 inches above the floor.

- Grab bars placed at a 45-degree angle to the toilet or in the bathtub may be easier for people to reach. An angled 24-inch grab bar perfectly spans wall studs spaced 16 inches apart for extra support.

Privacy

The most accessible bathrooms typically are open, with few interior dividers. Yet creating a barrier-free bath doesn't mean sacrificing privacy—it just requires some creativity.

The bathroom is a private retreat. Where you reside impacts how much privacy is required—if you live in a secluded area, window coverings aren't as important as they are when a street or neighbor's window is within view. To create privacy without blocking the natural light windows provide, install glass block or frosted or stained-glass windows. If you opt for window treatments, select quick-drying, washable fabrics that won't harbor mold and mildew. Blinds, shutters, and pull-down shades allow you to control the amount of light.

Sound Block

Acoustic privacy is another concern. To drown out the sound of flushing toilets, running showers, and other bathroom noises, install a ventilation fan (which also helps reduce the level of moisture in your bath). If you're remodeling, ask your contractor about insulating bathroom walls with noise-reducing wallboard and staggered, spaced framing with insulation.

Separate Spaces

In shared bathrooms, you may wish to create private areas, keeping in mind that a design with few internal walls or dividers is the most usable approach. If space allows, one solution is to install wide pocket doors that can be used to close off certain portions of the bath.

The toilet can be separated from the rest of the bath in a fully enclosed toilet room, in a nook, or behind a half-wall. A separate toilet room provides the most privacy but is the least accessible. Nooks or half-walls may be a better option because they provide a level of privacy without completely sacrificing access. There should be at least 18 inches of free space from the side wall to the center of the toilet. Install grab bars on the walls to the side of the toilet. If you do include a toilet compartment, it should have its own ventilation fan and a pocket door.

Photo courtesy of Kohler Co.

A half-wall creates a measure of seclusion for a toilet area without completely closing it off from the rest of the room.

Pocket doors, like
this mirrored unit, roll
smoothly on high-quality
ball-bearing tracks.
Pocket doors should
ideally be 36 inches wide
and have easy-to-reach
door hardware.

For shower or bath privacy, install a curtain
or shower walls of frosted glass or glass block,
which will obstruct views while still allowing
light to filter through.

Safety Tip

Include a phone jack in your bathroom wiring
plans near the tub, shower, and/or toilet.
That way, if necessary, help is just a phone
call away.

A curved wall of glass block provides privacy for
bathers while allowing light to filter through.

Vanities & Countertops

Well-designed vanities function as more than a place for hand washing and storage. Quality countertops and cabinetry are durable and make your bathroom an appealing space.

Vanities present unique design challenges, particularly if the people accessing the sink include household members of different heights or those who wish to sit on a stool or bench while washing or grooming. One option for accommodating a variety of users is to include two sinks at different heights. In general, mounting a countertop at 34 to 36 inches is best for standing; 32 to 34 inches is ideal for seated users. Tall individuals may benefit from a countertop that's 38 to 43 inches.

Set the sink into the vanity or countertop as close to the front edge as possible to minimize reaching. If the sink will be used from a seated position, plan for leg room of 27 to 29 inches high by 32 to 36 inches wide by 19 inches deep beneath the sink. For safety, the pipes beneath the sink should be set as far back as possible and covered with insulation or a protective panel to guard against burns.

Countertop Choices

Solid-surface materials can be made into countertops with rounded edges for safety and with integral sinks for easy cleaning. Countertop edges in a contrasting color are helpful for people with limited vision. Glare is an important factor, too—matte finishes are best for people who are sensitive to bright light.

Beyond these general guidelines, consider your style and budget. Take into account ease of cleaning and how well each material withstands wear—the goal should be a countertop material that will stay beautiful and functional for as long as you're in your home. (Learn more about countertop materials on pages 34–35.)

Beneath the Sink

Making a vanity accessible for seated users may mean dedicating some space to undercounter storage. If the vanity is wide enough, you may be able to have drawers or cabinets on either side of the sink. Choose cabinet and drawer hardware that is easy to grasp and pull. (Learn more about bathroom storage on pages 70–73.)

Sturdy stools provide little ones access to this playful wall-mount vanity area. Colorful sinks and single-lever faucets help kids clean up and brush teeth on their own.

Photo courtesy of Kohler Co.

Photo courtesy of Kohler Co.

A vanity mounted directly to the wall and a sink that comes to the edge of the countertop provide attractive, easy access for seated users.

Kid-Friendly Bathrooms

Rubber duckies and other fun decor may make bathrooms more welcoming for children, but they don't help make adult-sized bath fixtures easier for little ones to use. For safety and ease, consider the following:

- Keep a sturdy step stool in the bathroom so children can reach the sink and see into the mirror on their own.

- Hang hooks and shelves that store children's items within reach.

- Designate an area for storing bath toys so they aren't left strewn about the floor and the tub (a danger for kids and adults).

- Make sure items such as blow dryers and electric razors are stored away from water sources and out of children's reach.

- Keep medicines and cleaning products in a locked cabinet (or better yet, in another room that children don't use).

Installing child-size bathroom fixtures can be expensive because you usually have to replace them within a few years. If you are considering them, especially for a child with a disability, the ADA guidelines for toilet and grab bar heights for children are available at **www.usdoj.gov/crt/ada/stdspdf.htm**

Safety Tip

Items that are regularly used in the bathroom often remain on the vanity countertop. For safety, use unbreakable cups, soap dishes, and other accessories. Set hair dryers, curling irons, and electric razors away from the sink and other bathroom water sources, and unplug them when not in use.

Sinks & Faucets

The right sink and faucet make a big difference in comfort and usability. Style, ease of use, and your budget all figure into the equation as well.

Bathroom sinks get plenty of use, which means it's important to select the best fixture and faucet for your situation. Common sink materials include porcelain-enameled cast iron, vitreous china, and solid-surfacing. Porcelain-enameled cast-iron sinks are popular because they are durable and easy to care for.

Wall-mount sinks can fit into tight spaces and can be installed at any height, providing clear space underneath for seated users. This type of sink should be installed with heavy-duty brackets or extra bracing so it doesn't pull loose from the wall if someone leans on it.

Console sinks (see the image at the top of page 68) are an attractive option; the legs that support the sink are spaced far enough apart to allow room underneath for seated users, although the plumbing pipes should be protected for safety. Vanity sinks typically provide countertop space as well as storage (or leg room) below. See the opposite page for specific information on vanity sink styles.

Pedestal sinks are the least accessible option. They sit atop a center base, which offers little counterspace and no base cabinet storage or leg room for seated users. If you like the look of pedestal sinks, they're best suited for non-essential powder rooms that receive little traffic.

Look for a sink with a drain at the back that allows pipes to be installed out of the way. If possible, choose a sink that's shallower at the front. Sinks that jut beyond the countertop provide easier access when users are seated. Larger, deeper sinks reduce splashing and countertop cleanup—but consider the fact that the faucet should be within 21 inches of the front of the vanity for easier reach.

Also remember to leave at least 18 inches of clearance from the centerline of the sink to the closest wall so there's elbow room; if you are including two sinks side by side on a vanity, leave at least 30 inches of clearance between the centerlines of each.

Faucet Flow

Sink faucets typically mount on the fixture itself or next to it on the countertop. Wall-mount

Photo courtesy of Pressalit Care

Adjustable sinks that move vertically are an alternative to vanities at set heights. A height-adjustment mechanism allows this specialized sink to move to fit the needs of each user with minimal effort.

faucets are often used with vessel-shape sinks—this looks beautiful, but the faucet usually is set too far back to comfortably accommodate seated users. A single-lever faucet is easier to use than double handles for most people, because the water temperature and strength of the water flow can be controlled with one hand. Installing a faucet with a motion sensor assists users even more.

Sink Styles

Vanity sinks can be installed in several ways, depending on the sink style you select. The most common styles are described below:

- **Self-rimming or surface-mount** sinks are dropped into the counter. They're the easiest type of sink to install, can be paired with a variety of countertop materials, and may be replaced without damaging the countertop. The seam where the rim of the sink meets the countertop is tightly sealed with caulk; be sure to keep the seam clean.

- **Undermount** sinks are attached below the countertop, providing a seamless sink and countertop connection. The countertop material used with undermount sinks should be waterproof, such as stone or solid-surfacing.

- **Integral** sinks are formed as one unit with the vanity countertop. They are easy to clean because there isn't a joint between the bowl and the countertop, but if the sink or countertop is damaged, both have to be replaced.

- **Vessel** sinks fit in a custom-cut hole in the vanity top. They provide an elegant design statement but can be difficult to use while seated if the vessel sits too high on the countertop. Many vessel sinks require wall-mount faucets and specialized drainpipe fittings.

Single-lever faucets and surface-mount sinks make a striking pair. This type of faucet is easy to operate.

Tubs & Showers

Spa-like luxuries, including whirlpool jets and body-mist shower sprays, can be incorporated with safety and convenience features in modern tubs and showers. This makes it possible for people of all ages and physical abilities to bathe in comfort.

Many accidents occur in and around tubs and showers because water and hard surfaces create slippery situations. A separate shower and tub may be the most convenient, comfortable, and safe over the long run.

For safety in both tubs and showers, install grab bars and choose a matte, textured, or other nongloss finish for the floor. In tubs and showers, place nonslip rubber suction mats or bath appliqués for secure footing. If space allows, include a seat 17 to 19 inches high and at least 15 inches deep. Seat styles include built-in benches in the shower, portable stools with nonslip feet, and transfer seats (which help people with limited mobility get into the tub).

Tubs

Tub styles include recessed, corner, platform, and freestanding. When purchasing a tub, consider how easy it will be for bathers to get in and out. It may be more difficult to climb into a recessed or freestanding tub than it is to slide into a platform model that has a wide, flat tub surround. Another option is to purchase a walk-in tub with an easy-access door (as shown on this page); however, keep in mind that users have to sit in the tub while filling and draining, which can be chilly.

Regardless of tub type, there should be clear floor space of at least 36×60 inches in front of

the tub. If you use a shower curtain for privacy, make sure the rod is securely attached to the wall, as bathers may grab it to prevent a fall.

A walk-in tub with a low-step entrance facilitates easy entry and exit from the bath.

This barrier-free shower includes a hand-held shower sprayer, fold-up seat, grab bars, and a slip-resistant, textured floor for safety.

A beautiful platform tub with a wide surround allows users to sit on the edge, then slide into the tub. The deck-mount sprayer aids with washing hair or rinsing off.

Photo courtesy of Kohler Co.

Position water controls and faucets so they are easy to reach from inside and outside the tub at a height of 38 to 48 inches above the floor so the water can be adjusted before bathers get in; offsetting the controls toward the open side of the tub allows easy reach. Installing a hand-held shower sprayer in addition to a fixed faucet makes rinsing off easier. A cushion installed on the tub spout helps prevent cuts and bruises.

Showers

Tubs are a nice luxury if space permits, but in smaller bathrooms with room for only one bathing fixture, a shower is a more practical choice. Showers come in single or multipiece units or may be custom-built. At a minimum, they should measure 4 feet square with an opening at least 32 inches wide. Purchase the largest shower unit that will fit well in your bath. Shower stalls that are 60 inches wide increase comfort and usability by providing additional maneuvering space and room for someone to assist a bather if necessary. A curbless shower without doors or a curtain is easiest to get into; just be certain the shower floor slopes toward the drain so water stays within the enclosure. If you opt for a door on the shower, look for one that opens out for easier access.

Shower controls should be mounted between the showerhead and the stall door so they can be accessed from outside the shower. A single-lever water control is easiest to use. To make bathing easier whether you are seated or standing, include a hand-held shower spray with a 72-inch-long hose, an on/off control on the showerhead, and a soft spray option to protect sensitive skin. A vertical track that lets the bather move the shower head up and down to the desired position allows for hands-free showering; just be sure the track doesn't get in the way of grab bar placement.

Steam Showers & Saunas

The health benefits of steam showers and saunas range from relieving stress and cleansing the body to soothing aching muscles and joints. With a bit of planning, you can install a sauna or a steam shower in your master bath.

Steam showers and saunas provide similar benefits; the main difference is that saunas produce a dry, desert-like heat, while steam showers produce moist heat.

Steam Showers

Purchasing a shower stall equipped to handle steam or retrofitting a current stall are two options for acquiring a steam shower. If your shower is not a prefabricated acrylic or fiberglass unit with a sealed door, you'll need to modify it for a watertight enclosure. Be sure to install a vapor barrier on the ceiling and wall framing to prevent moisture from reaching studs and joists.

Steam showers operate from a small generator located outside the enclosure, which sends steam into the shower through a pipe. The generator capacity should match the size and type of the shower enclosure. You can use a shower outfitted for steam for standard bathing or deliver the benefits of steam with the push of a button.

Saunas

Saunas can require minimal space—many small closets provide enough room for a sauna heater and bench—or they can be large enough to accommodate multiple users. You can have a sauna installed in your bath with a prefabricated or custom kit, or have one

Spa-Like Amenities

To take the spa experience even further, consider including these amenities in your bath:

- Hydromassage tubs that use jets to soothe aching muscles.
- Chromatherapy showers, which feature fiber-optic lights to cast colors—some hues relax, others invigorate.
- Aromatherapy bath oils and candles to increase relaxation while bathing.

custom-made. Much like steam showers, saunas require a vapor barrier so heat can't escape. Ventilation is important, too, in order to keep the oxygen levels up and help distribute heat. Saunas may be heated with electric or gas heaters or infrared-emitting lights. Consider which method will be most convenient for you.

Photo courtesy of Kohler Co.

For a spa-like addition to your bath, consider a shower with a sealed door that functions as a steam shower, too.

The toilet presents unique universal design challenges. Fortunately, new toilet models combine comfort and convenience in a package made to fit even small spaces.

Toilets

Like any bathroom fixture, toilets come in a variety of styles. Raised-height, wall-hung, and in-wall tank toilets are the most accessible. Although they are only a couple of inches taller than standard toilets, raised-height models (which may be 17 to 19 inches tall) have a big impact on ease of use for many people. The exception: a raised-height model that is 19 inches or higher may be too tall to comfortably accommodate children or many adults. In this case, an adjustable-height toilet or a model with a power-lift seat may be a better option. A seat that adds 2 to 5 inches in height to a standard toilet or one that offers two different heights—to accommodate adults and children with the same seat—are other possibilities.

A kid seat nestles inside an adult seat atop this toilet, making it easy to use for family members of all sizes.

Photo courtesy of Kohler Co.

A wall-mount toilet takes up less space than standard models and is easier to clean. Here, a cushion attached to the wall adds a level of comfort.

Photo courtesy of Pressalit Care

Toilet Placement

A toilet is easiest to access when it is situated in the corner of a 5×5-foot space with a grab bar affixed to the wall 18 inches from the centerline of the toilet. Remember to install grab bars around the toilet or, if not needed now, install broad bands of reinforcing to the wall beside and behind the toilet so you can add them later. Toilet seats with grab bars attached are another option for people with limited mobility. Because they're easily removable, the seats may be affixed to the toilet when you have visitors who need assistance.

Space-Saving Options

Wall-mount toilets can be installed at any height. Because there is no toilet base, this type offers more space around the toilet and makes cleaning easier. Another option is an in-wall tank toilet, which opens up more space because everything but the bowl portion of the toilet is installed behind the wall. Both of these toilets mount to the wall framing.

Toilet bowl shape also influences how much space a toilet requires. Round-front bowls fit better in smaller spaces, but elongated toilets are more comfortable for sitting and may be worth the additional inches they require.

Flooring

Safety is paramount when it comes to bathroom floors, but this need not limit your style. New flooring materials offer many choices.

Nonslip flooring is vital in bathrooms. Look for the COF (or coefficient of friction), the measure of how slip-resistant the surface is. A COF of 0.6 or higher is best. In addition, look for flooring materials that are glare-free.

Area rugs can cause falls and injuries, so it's best to avoid using them in the bathroom. If you prefer the warmth of a rug on bare feet, make certain it has rubber backing so it's less likely to slide when you stand on it.

Flooring Materials

Resilient flooring is recommended for bathrooms rather than colder, harder materials such as ceramic tile. Slip-resistant sheet vinyl or nonskid textured vinyl in a light color is a good option. This type of flooring is cushioned, so it helps muffle noise and is easy on feet and legs. Another resilient flooring option (as long as it doesn't have a glossy finish) is laminate, which provides the look of tile or wood for less money, stands up to water and wear, and is relatively maintenance-free.

If you opt for ceramic tile in the bathroom, purchase small tiles glazed with a nonslip finish. Covering a floor with small tiles requires more grout, which further increases slip-resistance. Mildew-proof carpeting is another option, although it makes traveling through the bathroom more difficult for those using a wheelchair or walker. (Learn more about flooring materials on pages 42–43.)

Heated Flooring

Radiant-heating systems use hot water to keep feet warm. You may choose to install a hydronic—or water-based—system throughout your home. However, if you just want a warmer floor in the bath, electric systems are easier and less expensive to install. They use thin, flat cables installed under ceramic-tile or stone flooring. The cables are connected to your home's electrical system and controlled by a thermostat.

Sheet vinyl's nonskid, waterproof construction makes it a smart choice for bathrooms. The earthy tone of this floor stylishly complements the wood cabinets and wall tiles.

Photo courtesy of Armstrong World Industries, Inc.

Walls are usually the largest surface in the bath. The right wall treatments can enhance your mood, add value to your home, and even make it easier to negotiate the space.

Walls & Color

Color influences mood and can make your bathroom safer when used correctly. Select wall colors that contrast with fixtures, countertops, and grab bars to make these items easier to see. If your walls and floors are light colors, darker grab bars are easily visible. If your bathroom fixtures are white, you may wish to paint the walls a darker color. Accessories, such as towels and toothbrush holders, are also easier to spot in colors that are distinctive from walls and countertops.

On the Walls

Paint, vinyl wall coverings, tile, and wood beadboard are common bathroom wall treatments. Paint is an inexpensive, low-maintenance option that is easy to change when you want a new look; washable and moisture-resistant paints are best. Vinyl wall coverings are a more durable choice for baths than regular wallpaper because they are scrubbable, withstand moisture, and are easy to adhere to the wall. With its variety

of patterns, colors, and textures, tile can be worth the cost because of its longevity. Another option: wood beadboard sealed with water-resistant coating adds natural warmth to almost any style of bath.

Color Smarts

Colors help create a mood in your living spaces. To make your bath a soothing retreat or an energizing oasis, consider these palette pointers:

- Use color sparingly for a peaceful bath. An all-neutral color scheme brings about feelings of safety and security.

- Opt for cool colors, such as blue, for calm and serenity.

- Colors that are prominent in nature, such as green or beige, can be mixed with almost any color scheme.

- Choose warm hues, such as yellow, if you want a cheerful, energizing bath to help wake you up in the morning.

Photo courtesy of Kohler Co.

Photo courtesy of Kohler Co.

This shower is surrounded by small mosaic tiles (far left). Make sure tile is properly sealed.

A black toilet set against a white wall creates a pleasing contrast—and makes the fixture easier to see.

Lighting & Mirrors

The right combination of natural and artificial light and mirrors helps you see better, makes the bath appear more spacious, and can enhance your mood.

Lighting plays a role in the style and comfort of all rooms in the house, and it is particularly important for safety and grooming in the bathroom. Ideally, your bathroom lighting scheme should include windows as well as general overhead, task, safety, and accent lighting. Select light fixtures that are moisture-resistant, and outfit them with glare-free, full-spectrum lightbulbs, which produce truer light and are best for people with vision limitations.

Windows and Skylights

Operable windows are important for providing ventilation in a bathroom. The more natural light that fills your bath, the more welcoming it will be. Window treatments such as blinds or shades may be necessary for privacy and to reduce glare from surfaces like mirrors and countertops—particularly important for people whose eyes are sensitive to light. If options for window placement are limited, consider a

Shaded sconces flanking a mirror cast the perfect level of subdued light to illuminate a vanity area without glare.

Natural light, pendants, and recessed lights combine in this beautiful, well-lit bathroom. The large mirror above the vanity helps to visually extend the space.

Photo courtesy of Progress Lighting

Sconces near the vanity supplement the overhead and mirror lighting.

Safety Tip

Make certain all the electric receptacles in the bath are ground fault circuit interrupter-protected to reduce the risk of electrical shock. Install a circuit breaker GFCI to protect the entire circuit.

skylight or light tube. Motorized skylights and shades make it easy to adjust for ventilation and light.

Types of Light Fixtures

Bathroom lighting typically blends a number of fixtures. Recessed downlights, or "can" lights, are used for both general and task lighting. When used for general lighting, they should be close enough so their lighting patterns overlap. Wall sconces create ambient light and can work well for shadow-free task lighting when placed on each side of the mirror. Other task lighting options include pendant lights, track lights, and light bars.

A shower light is a good idea for safety. Most building codes require that shower fixtures be waterproof and steam-proof; enclosed, vapor-proof downlights are a good option. Install fixtures in the ceiling or high on the wall, where they illuminate the entire tub or shower without shining directly into your eyes.

Nightlights make nighttime trips to the bathroom easier and safer. Motion- or light-sensor models are available that plug into outlets. Look for LED lights, which last for years, use very little energy, and are dim enough not to shine too much light into adjacent bedrooms. Or install low-voltage wayfinding lights below a vanity toe-kick, around shelving, by grab bars, or embedded into walls and floors.

Lighting Controls

Rocker switches are the easiest for turning lights on and off; switches with built-in illumination can be located in the dark. Light controls should be installed at an easy-to-reach height 44 to 48 inches above the floor. Switches should ideally be at least 6 feet from tubs or showers.

Mirrors

Mirrors extend the lighting in a bathroom, help visually enlarge small spaces, and contribute to the bath's ambience. Full-length mirrors or mirrors that tilt or extend down to at least 40 inches from the floor allow children and people who are seated to see their reflections more easily. Vanity mirrors should be evenly illuminated and shadow-free. To achieve this, install a fixture above the mirror to cast light over the front edge of the sink or countertop, and place additional lights at eye level on each side of the mirror. Light-colored countertops help reflect light on your face even more.

Storage Solutions

Toiletries and towels are just a few of the items stored in the bathroom. With the right combination of shelves, cabinets, drawers, and more, everything that belongs in your bath will have its own easily accessible spot.

The most accessible storage plan for a bathroom combines open and closed storage at different heights. Open storage such as shelving or niches makes reaching items easier because doors aren't in the way, while closed storage keeps clutter out of sight and items out of reach of young children. Some of the storage in a bathroom should be positioned low enough for seated users and children to access; less frequently used items may be stored on higher shelves or in cabinets.

Broad, shallow shelves allow users to access items easily. Adjustable shelves accommodate changing storage needs. Use baskets and trays to corral clutter on open shelves if necessary.

Cabinets of varying heights accommodate family members of different sizes. If you have a

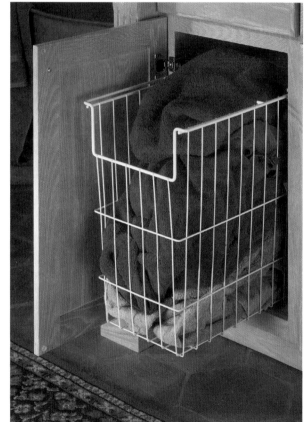

Cabinets outfitted with pull-out baskets are ideal for tossing used towels (once they've dried) or dirty clothes.

Position this cabinet next to the bathtub and you'll have a spot for placing items within reach of bathers.

Photo courtesy of Robern

This medicine cabinet features a soft blue LED light that automatically turns on in low-light conditions.

cabinet above the vanity, make sure it is at an accessible height. Roll-out base cabinets also provide storage that is easy for seated users to access. Low cabinets with pull-out shelves or bins are another option for toiletries, trash receptacles, or laundry hampers. Also consider built-in hutches or freestanding pieces if you have a large bath.

Hardware

Two types of hardware are important in bathrooms. The first includes sturdy towel bars and hooks mounted on the wall for hanging towels, robes, and other items. Towel bars or rings may also be mounted on the front or side of a vanity so they are within reach of seated users. Or affix attractive grab bars to the front of the vanity below the countertop and above doors or open knee space instead—they can serve as hand holds for people with balance problems and double as towel bars.

The second type of hardware is found on cabinets and includes hinges, knobs, and handles. Magnetic-touch and push-and-release catches on cabinet doors make them easier to open and close. Or consider sliding doors, which are easier to use because they don't swing open into available leg room. Large, easy-to-grasp pulls or knobs make opening cabinets easier.

Safety Tip

In family baths or any bathroom that children may use, install childproof locks on medicine cabinets. Designate a drawer where children can store their own bathroom items, and keep all the rest out of reach or locked up.

Storing Medicine

As their name implies, medicine cabinets are often used for storing medication in the bathroom. But should you actually store your prescriptions there?

The answer is no, according to Kasey Thompson, Pharm.D., director of patient safety for the American Society of Health-System Pharmacists.

"A very basic rule of thumb is that medications should never be stored in the bathroom because of the negative effects of excessive heat and humidity," Thompson says. "Medicines should ideally be stored in a secure, dark location at 65 to 80 degrees, with little humidity."

In addition, Thompson recommends asking your pharmacist if medications you are taking require special storage considerations, such as refrigeration.

Instead of stashing your prescriptions in the bathroom cabinet, use that space to store bandages, toothbrushes and toothpaste, and other toiletries that aren't negatively affected by heat and humidity.

Pull-out baskets mounted under the counter allow you to easily grab frequently used items, such as washcloths.

Photo courtesy of Pressalit Care

© Bob Greenspan, photo courtesy of Mascord

Photo courtesy of Baldwin Hardware Corporation

Position towel bars near the shower or tub for easy access after bathing. A decorative shelf adds a touch of style and extra storage in this bath.

Closed undercounter storage keeps clutter out of sight. Some vanities hide open knee space beneath the sink behind cabinet doors that slide or fold out of the way.

Waterproof caddies attached to the toilet and shower seats keep toiletries such as hand sanitizer and shampoo within reach.

A rolling cart that stashes towels and other bathing supplies can be moved around the bath as needed and pushed beneath an open vanity when not in use.

An undercounter drawer keeps beauty products organized right where they're needed—and still allows seated users to pull up beneath the sink.

Cost Estimates

Bathroom Remodeling

Like kitchens, baths are excellent candidates for adding universal design features if you're planning to remodel or update the space. But even without major renovations, support bars, hand-held shower sprayers, toilet modifications, and new light and plumbing fixtures can be added fairly easily.

This estimate shows what it will cost to totally remodel a basic, three-fixture bath to include universal design features that will accommodate everyone, including people who use wheelchairs. Costs include labor and materials to remove the old bath fixtures, wall and floor coverings, and to install new, accessible fixtures and fittings, along with nonslip tile flooring and tile walls. The estimate includes a few specialty items such as a folding shower seat, support bars, an anti-scald device, and a tilted mirror. Costs include contractor's labor and overhead and are based on national averages.

Estimate Breakdown

Bathroom remodel to include all required demolition and disconnections, an allowance for some framing and blocking, insulation, drywall, ceramic tile on walls and floor, and painting and finishing.	$6,500.00
Plumbing to include installation of a new lavatory (sink), water closet (toilet), and accessible shower.	$2,600.00
Electrical work to include wiring, switches, receptacles, and light fixtures.	$600.00
Demolition debris removal (dumpster)	$875.00
Sub-total	**$10,575.00**
(Add local sales tax for total)	

Other Cost Factors:

- Additional rough-in piping if you're changing the layout of fixtures, especially if moving them to a new wall.

- Possible water heater upgrade if you install a whirlpool tub that doesn't have its own heater and uses more water than a standard tub—and additional framing to support a large tub if the weight exceeds 30 pounds per square foot when filled.

- Reframing walls to enlarge or re-partition the space.

A barrier-free shower with grab bars makes entering and exiting the area easier and safer. The shower floor should slope toward the drain so water stays within the shower enclosure.

Flooring Options

Costs per Square Foot Installed	
Pre-finished oak strip	$10.70
Floating laminate	$9.00
Sheet vinyl	$8.25
Vinyl tiles	$6.05
Ceramic tile	$12.95
³/₈" Particleboard underlayment	$2.25

Return on Investment

New and remodeled baths, along with kitchens, are the biggest contributors to a home's resale value. The more out-of-date the old bath, the more value a renovation will bring. Value is also influenced by the quality of workmanship and materials and a neutral style and color scheme.

Permanently installed universal design features such as support bars should be attractive and blend with the decor, standing out as little as possible. Other recommended features, such as open floor space and wide doorways, will be appreciated by nearly everyone. Items such as toilet height extenders and portable shower and tub seats can be removed when not needed or to show a house if and when you decide to put it on the market.

5

Living Spaces

Whether you're relaxing, working, playing, or entertaining, odds are your living spaces are where you spend a good portion of your home life. From family and dining rooms to hobby areas and home offices, remember the importance of eliminating obstacles and selecting the right lighting—making these areas comfortable and safe. Add durable flooring, furnishings, and fabrics, and you're well on your way to creating attractive, easy-to-maintain living spaces that you and your family will love.

Floor Plan Basics

When designing a floor plan, consider not only where you'll place your favorite furniture and artwork, but also how you plan to use the space. Design flexible rooms that accommodate your family now and easily change with your needs.

A universally designed home should have an open floor plan that minimizes or eliminates barriers. Situating walls so rooms flow into one another ensures your home is easy to navigate, whether on foot or using a wheelchair.

A flexible, open floor plan maximizes the feeling of spaciousness in a home and allows you to experience the whole space visually without actually moving through it. This makes it easier to socialize with guests or keep an eye on children even when you're not in the same room. In addition, an open floor plan ensures you can adjust your home to fit changing needs.

Whether you are designing a home from scratch or remodeling, look for the best configuration for interior spaces. Minimizing walls and raising ceilings helps create a welcoming, expansive feel. Plan for an uncluttered pathway through each space at least 4 feet wide, if possible, to ensure people can easily maneuver. Also make room for a 5-foot turning diameter for people who use wheelchairs.

Think about the placement of elements including windows (sills no higher than 30 inches are best for viewing), lighting, and electrical outlets. Including plenty of windows provides optimum light, which makes it easier to navigate rooms. Depending on the room

Photo © Andersen Corporation

This open floor plan, which includes a living room and dining area open to the kitchen, is the ideal setup for a universally designed home. A wall of sliding glass doors ushers in ample natural light and takes advantage of stunning views.

Warm wood tones and varied textures pair for an inviting setting in this living room. An uncluttered pathway makes moving between furnishings easy.

Photo courtesy of Armstrong World Industries, Inc.

function and the exterior elevation, consider the need to use operable windows as exits in the event of fire or other emergency. Whenever possible, place items that require electricity directly in front of outlets so cords aren't a tripping hazard.

Living Spaces

Depending on the size of your home and your lifestyle, you may want a formal dining room and living room as well as an informal family room. When you design your floor plan, ask yourself how much you will use formal living spaces. If you often host guests for holidays or formal events and want a well-appointed space in which to entertain, perhaps formal dining and living areas are worthwhile. But if your family's lifestyle is more casual, consider replacing formal living spaces with a large living room and an eat-in kitchen instead. Better yet, break down barriers even further and create a great room that combines the family room, kitchen, and dining areas into one large space.

As you plan each of the following distinctive living spaces, remember that the primary goal is to create attractive, comfortable rooms that are

easy to access for anyone who might reside in or visit your home.

Family Rooms. Family, or great, rooms are typically flexible spaces that serve a variety of functions—from watching TV and movies to reading, playing games, doing homework, or relaxing. As you plan yours, consider how your family uses the space now and how you might wish to use it in the future. For instance, now your family room may be a play area for your children or grandchildren, but later you may wish to turn it into a high-tech media room.

Regardless of its functions, your family room will work best if it is as spacious and open as possible. Include comfortable, durable

Photo courtesy of Armstrong World Industries, Inc.

A seating area that opens to the kitchen makes moving between rooms easy and facilitates conversation.

To provide space to navigate in a small dining room, consider using a round table with chairs. For alfresco dining, locate a door to the patio in your dining room or kitchen.

furnishings and materials. (Learn more about these on pages 84–87.) Storage for entertainment system components, DVDs, CDs, books, decorative items, and anything else important to you should be included as well. If you have a television in this area of your home, position it so reflected light from windows or light fixtures doesn't cause glare on the screen. Consider a fireplace for ambience and warmth.

Dining Rooms. If an open floor plan between the dining room and kitchen area isn't possible, make sure the doorway is wide. Open floor plans look best when the color and styles of adjoining rooms coordinate with each other.

Choose flooring that allows people to easily slide their chairs back from the table without scratching the surface.

Unless it is included as part of a great room, your dining area may have space restrictions. Include as big a table as will comfortably fit, making sure to leave a minimum of 48 inches between the table and the wall so there's room for people to move behind others who are seated. Leaving even more open space makes it easier for people to move around the table while

guests are seated. If someone using a wheelchair will regularly dine at this table, reserve an open spot with no dining chair.

Media Rooms. Televisions are usually located in the family or living room. Yet the noise can be distracting for people trying to read or work in a multi-purpose family room. One option is setting aside a specialized media room made for movie watching, game playing, and other forms of entertainment. Your media room may include a basic setup of television, DVD player, and speakers, or could have special seating, lighting, and a surround-sound system. To create the best viewing experience, locate seating away from the screen a distance of 2 to 2½ times the width of the screen; a head-on viewing angle is best. Be sure to store equipment on an open shelf or in a ventilated cabinet so it doesn't overheat. Look for electronics and remote controls with large buttons and easy-to-read labels. And to

A consistent color palette helps this formal dining room blend with the living room beyond. Wide, arched doorways open the space visually and make it easy to move from one area to another.

An L-shaped corner workstation is a fully functional office that takes up minimal space, which is particularly useful if your desk area is located in a family room or guest room.

avoid glare on the television screen, install dimmer light switches that provide control over the amount of artificial light in the room, and include window treatments that block sunshine.

Home Offices and Hobby Spaces. Whether you work from home or want a spot for bill paying and computer use, consider allotting space for a home office. For privacy, situate it away from high-traffic areas of your home. Or if peace and quiet aren't requirements while you work, include a desk area right in the family/great room or kitchen. Wireless Internet access allows you to use a laptop computer anywhere in the house.

Ergonomic design is an important consideration to minimize fatigue and strain on your body. Look for chairs and desks that fit you well. Ideally, your work surface should be at least 38 inches wide and 28 to 30 inches from the floor; allow for at least 27 inches from the floor to the underside of the desktop for leg clearance. Situating your desk approximately 34 inches from nearby walls, bookcases, or furniture ensures you have room to move back from your work surface. If you spend a lot of time at the computer, it's best to position your monitor at or just above eye level to prevent eye and neck strain. In addition, placing your keyboard slightly lower than your elbows (usually 25 to 29 inches above the floor) is best for avoiding carpal tunnel syndrome and other physical strain that comes from working at the keyboard for extended periods of time.

Pull-out keyboard trays and adjustable-height chairs with lower-back support may be pricier than standard models, but if you spend long periods of time at your desk, they are likely worth the investment. Consider purchasing cabinets with wheels to store printers and other office equipment; this allows you to

Ample storage and a U-shape layout combines an office with a hobby space.

Consider locating an office area in or near the family room for convenience. A rug helps visually distinguish this desk area from the living spaces around it.

easily move them closer to your desk when needed. Store items on pull-out shelves and use file cabinets that open smoothly and easily. Heavy items, such as large books and baskets of craft supplies, should be placed on easy-to-reach shelves to eliminate bending too low or reaching overhead.

If you enjoy pastimes such as scrapbooking, sewing, or painting, you may wish to include a hobby room in your home. Or consider a craft corner right in your family room or spare bedroom. For pursuits that take up more space, such as woodworking, carve out space in a garage or backyard shed.

Much like kitchens, home offices and hobby rooms function best with layouts that accommodate the way you work. Consider whether a one-wall, L-shaped, two-wall, or U-shaped setup works best for your needs.

Exercise Rooms. Depending on available space, an exercise room might include weight machines, free weights, a treadmill or elliptical machine, and perhaps open floor space for stretching or doing yoga. Floor-to-ceiling mirrors allow you to watch

Converting Basements and Attics

The best layout for a universally designed home places all living areas on a single floor. Yet many homes include attics, basements, or both—and who wants to let all that space go to waste? To take advantage of all the square footage your home has to offer, keep these ideas in mind:

- **Place** guest bedrooms, baths, and playrooms on upper- and lower-level floors if most of your guests (perhaps children and grandchildren) are younger and able-bodied.

- **Keep** your main living spaces uncluttered by using basements and attics for storage—but beware that hauling items from these areas may be difficult and even dangerous without help.

- **Ensure** that stairways meet universal design recommendations. (See pages 24–25.) In particular, stairways should not be too steep and should have handrails on both sides.

- **Consider** safety. Habitable rooms should have a window square footage that measures 10 percent of the room's total square footage; for ventilation, at least half of the window area should be operable windows, or other ventilation options must be used. All sleeping rooms should have a door or window through which people can exit in case of emergency. Exterior stairs from attic escape windows may not be required, but keep a flexible emergency ladder nearby.

Photo © James A. Stepp

Ample lighting is important for safety in an exercise room. Here tall windows supplement artificial lighting.

your form while weightlifting. If you don't have an entire room to dedicate to fitness, consider making space for a treadmill or free weights in a spare bedroom, the garage, or an out-of-the-way corner of the family room. Make certain all electric fitness equipment has safety keys or switches so children can't turn them on without adult supervision.

With durable flooring and access to the outdoors, this lower-level room makes the perfect play space—as long as children are able to climb the stairs safely on their own.

Photo courtesy of Armstrong World Industries, Inc.

Fabrics & Furnishings

Furnishings and fabrics complete the room. Look for sturdy, comfortable pieces that are touchable, attractive, and easily maintained.

Decorating your home with furnishings, fabrics, and accessories is, of course, very much a matter of personal taste. But if you wish to create a home that is comfortable for people of all ages and physical abilities, consider these easy living design ideas.

Furniture

Well-designed furniture is worth the investment. Comfortable, durable seating will last for many years and make your living spaces much more inviting. Furniture that isn't designed properly may be uncomfortable and even cause back pain.

In particular, furniture made for seating should accommodate people of all sizes and mobility levels. Chairs and sofas with sturdy arms and firm seats that aren't too low or deep and don't rock or swivel are best. Plush seating may seem comfortable, but it can make getting up difficult and may not provide the support your body needs. Instead, select a firmer seat and choose

Photo courtesy of Sunbrella

Arrange furniture to optimize natural light. This soft, upholstered chair with a matching ottoman is perfect for curling up with a book in a well-lit corner.

Photo © Andersen Corporation

soft, upholstered fabrics and throw pillows for added comfort.

Furniture that fits comfortably should allow your knees to bend at the edge of the seat (look for a seat depth of 20 inches and a seat height of 18 to 20 inches), provide a level of support for your neck and back, and have wide armrests that are sturdy enough for you to use as support as you move to sit down or stand up. Reclining chairs reduce stress on your lower back and allow you to elevate your feet. But recliners can be difficult for people with limited leg strength to operate, so choose one with an easy-to-use mechanism. Special lifting seats can help people stand and sit.

When selecting new furnishings such as ottomans, tables, and bookshelves, look for rounded corners—an especially important safety feature for hard surfaces like coffee and side tables. Look for multi-purpose furnishings, such as an ottoman that serves as a footrest and additional seating with a bonus like storage inside, or a sofa with a pull-out bed.

Firm yet comfortable furnishings upholstered in durable fabrics are a smart choice for living rooms. Neutral-color couches and chairs work with almost any decorating scheme.

Arranging Furniture

Choose furnishings that are the proper scale— oversized pieces may be comfortable, but too many large-scale furnishings can make it hard to navigate through the room. In addition, remove unnecessary furnishings and look for lightweight pieces that are easy to move around should you want to rearrange or move them aside for cleaning or entertaining.

Safety Tip

Certain window treatments may be dangerous, particularly if young children are present. Eliminate dangling cords by gathering them out of reach. Many alternatives to cord-operated window treatments are available. Look for cordless horizontal and vertical blinds, pleated shades, roll-up fabric shades, and wood blinds operated by remote control. Blinds and shades installed between panels of glass eliminate cords and the risk that children might pull on the window treatments as well. Spring-loaded cellular shades are another option: simply push or pull the center of the bottom rail handle to raise or lower them with minimal effort.

Photo courtesy of Fabrica

This dining table with chairs is situated in a great room where there is plenty of space for navigating around the table.

Fabrics

Fabrics are a welcome addition to living spaces because they provide color, pattern, and texture. Selecting the right fabrics can enhance the style and comfort of your rooms. Which material you ultimately choose to upholster your furnishings, cover pillows, and hang from windows will depend on your decorating scheme and personal tastes. But there are a few design tips worth considering.

Look for fabrics that are durable, stain- and fade-resistant, water-repellent, and easy to completely clean (particularly in homes with young children). Avoid solid, light-color fabrics on furnishings such as sofas that sustain a lot of use. Opt for subtly textured materials on

One way to create a universal floor plan—particularly for people who use walkers or wheelchairs and for families with young children who need floor space for play—is to move all furniture against the walls, which maximizes available space in the center of the room for moving and turning. Should you wish to have more intimate conversation areas, however, it's still possible to arrange items in an easily navigable fashion. Just be sure to leave clear, wide pathways so people with mobility or vision problems—or anyone, for that matter—can safely and easily move through a room. A minimum of 38 inches clearance is recommended to accommodate passage around and through groupings of furniture.

Photo courtesy of Conrad Imports Inc.

Natural, hand-woven window treatments allow diffuse light to enter living spaces while reducing glare. Curtains may be pulled to block even more light for napping or watching television.

A few well-appointed furnishings are all that's needed to make this living room accommodating and still leave plenty of open floor space.

seating rather than slippery fabrics, which can make it difficult for people to sit comfortably. But avoid fabrics that are too coarse or textured if you or someone who will frequent your home has particularly sensitive skin.

Have fun with the materials you select for window treatments and throw pillows, which needn't be as durable as upholstery or slipcover fabrics. You can play with pattern and color as well—just be aware that too many busy patterns can be distracting for people with vision problems and may overwhelm small spaces.

Quality Furnishings

When shopping, look for these signs of high-quality furniture:

Wood pieces should be solid, with smooth surfaces, evenly applied finishes, and matching wood grain (e.g., across table leaves and drawer fronts). Dense wood resists scratching, staining, and denting better than soft woods. Hardware should be solid and operate quietly and smoothly. Drawers should glide easily.

Quality upholstered furniture is solid, not wobbly or squeaky. Seams and cording (welt) should be even, with no gaps. Hand-tied coil springs support areas that get the most stress, like chair seats and backs. Sofas and chairs should be padded on every surface for comfort and to keep fabric from wearing.

Flooring

The flooring materials you choose for your living spaces will depend on the function and style of each room. Select flooring that is durable yet comfortable underfoot for high-traffic areas.

Hard surfaces are smart flooring options for a universal home because they facilitate movement, particularly for people who use wheelchairs or walkers. Wood, ceramic, vinyl, and laminate flooring are often used throughout the house—just make sure they have a nonslip, matte finish.

Comfort is important—particularly in living spaces—so if you plan to walk around barefoot or sprawl out on the floor on occasion, you may want to include area rugs. Rugs are also useful for delineating seating areas. Just make certain they are low-pile and affixed to the floor so they won't slip, and avoid rugs with bold patterns and colors, which may be visually distracting.

Hardwood or durable wood-look laminate is attractive in living areas. Low-pile rugs add comfort.

Photo courtesy of Fabrica

Photo courtesy of Mohawk Industries

Many homeowners install carpet instead of harder surfaces because of its warmth. Another bonus: carpeting on floors reduces sharp noises and distracting echoes. Like area rugs, wall-to-wall carpet should be tight-loop and low-pile with a thin pad for easy transitions between different types of flooring.

Select tight-loop carpeting rather than thick, plush varieties to enjoy the warmth without sacrificing ease of movement.

Paint, wallpaper, or other decorative treatments not only affect the feeling of the space, but can enhance visibility.

Wall Treatments

The options for wall treatments are almost endless. You can paint all of the walls a single neutral hue; brush a bold color on an accent wall; or adorn the walls with decorative paint techniques such as sponging, stenciling, stamping, and glazing. Paint is generally easy to apply and low-commitment—should you decide you don't like the color you chose, you can repaint.

Wallpaper can be applied as a border or to an entire wall and can even help to absorb sound and minimize background noise, a plus if someone in your home has difficulty hearing. Opt for small patterns that aren't too busy—otherwise the patterns may make it difficult for people who have trouble seeing to navigate the room. (Learn more about paint and wallpaper treatments on page 107.)

In addition to adding architectural detail to walls, moldings serve a variety of functions in the home. Strategically placed chair rails are popular in new homes because they provide support much like handrails do while blending into a room's decor. Plate rails, located higher on the wall, can be used to display breakable items where they can't be knocked over easily. Paneling on the lower part of walls is another possibility, especially in more formal areas, such as dining or living rooms, where it protects from wear and tear.

Safe Paint

Few things brighten living spaces quite as quickly or easily as paint. But many paint products negatively impact the air quality of your home. According to the Environmental Protection Agency (EPA), paints, stains, and other architectural coatings are a major producer of volatile organic compound (VOC) emissions. VOCs don't just harm the environment; they can cause respiratory, skin, and eye irritation; nausea; muscle weakness; and more serious health problems. And formaldehyde, which is commonly found in paint, is a probable carcinogen.

The good news is that there are plenty of good-quality low- or no-VOC paints on the market, which reduce the amount of VOCs you are exposed to during and after application. (For even more assurance, purchase paints certified by Green Seal.)

Photo © Bob Greenspan; courtesy of Mascord

A decorative paint treatment, a picture rail, wood wainscoting, and a wood and tile fireplace surround lend architectural style to this sitting area.

Color

Color can greatly enhance your living spaces, making them warm and welcoming or cool and soothing depending on your tastes and the light in the room. Choosing the right hues can also make it easier to see and navigate spaces.

Adding color to the rooms in your home is a relatively easy endeavor—paint the walls, hang vibrant artwork, include colorful fabrics and furnishings, and you're set. Picking the right hues, however, can be a bit tricky. Here's help.

Color Basics

Color is the by-product of the spectrum of light as it is reflected or absorbed. Visible light is made of seven wavelength groups—red, orange, yellow, green, blue, indigo, and violet. Red has the longest wavelength and violet the shortest. The progression of color from largest to shortest wavelength is usually presented in a color wheel with 12 hues. Colors on opposite sides of the wheel create *complementary* color schemes; colors adjacent to one another are used for *analogous* schemes. A *triadic* scheme

Photo © Andersen Corporation

Yellow walls help extend the mood of sunny outdoor spaces indoors. Crisp white trim around the doors provides pleasing contrast.

Photo courtesy of Sherwin-Williams

White furnishings stand out against a bold red wall. The juxtaposition of dark against light colors makes it easier for people who have vision problems to see where two surfaces meet.

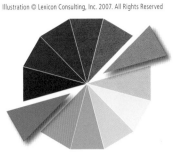

Analogous   Complementary

A color wheel shows the relationship between colors and can be helpful for selecting room color schemes.

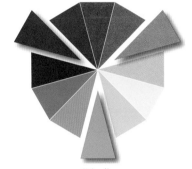

Triadic

Color greatly affects mood. Green, for instance, is a soothing color that has been shown to help alleviate depression and anxiety.

uses three colors equally spaced around the color wheel. And shades and tints of a single hue create a *monochromatic* color scheme.

Color and Mood

Color helps set the mood in a room, so the first step in selecting the main colors to use in your living spaces is to determine what mood you want. Reds, oranges, and yellows convey warmth. Watery blues and greens are cooler and soothing. Bolder, brighter colors have more energy than lighter, restful shades.

Color Smarts

Use of color should be a consideration in your universally designed home. Contrast is important, particularly for people with vision problems, helping the elements of a room stand out. It's hard to distinguish items in a room decorated with closely related colors, but hues on opposite sides of the color wheel are more likely to pop when they're next to one another. In particular, use contrast to distinguish doorways from walls (perhaps with bright

white trimwork and darker wall colors) and furnishings from flooring (try neutral carpeting and colorful upholstery fabrics).

Lighting and Color

The lighting in your home may affect the appearance of certain colors. It's a good idea to get large samples of the paint, wallpaper, and fabrics you're considering. Take them home to see how they look in natural and artificial light before making a decision.

The way colors look in your room may depend on the position of the sun. Northern exposures may have bluer, cooler light, while southern exposures have warmer, yellowish tones. Light fixtures play a part, too—incandescent bulbs emphasize red and yellow hues, while some fluorescent bulbs highlight blue tones. Base your decisions on how the colors look in the rooms where they'll be used at all times of day and night.

Lighting

It doesn't matter how you design your living spaces if there isn't enough illumination to enjoy them. Your lighting plan should incorporate a variety of light sources to ensure safety, comfort, attractiveness, and efficiency.

A smart lighting design incorporates three basic types of artificial light: general ambient illumination, task lighting, and accent lighting for decorative effect. Uniform lighting levels throughout the home ensure there aren't any dark, shadowy areas.

Lighting Styles

There are a number of options available for supplementing the ambient lighting provided by overhead fixtures. Remember that each functional area within a larger room should have its own task lighting.

Mounted on the ceiling, track lighting helps eliminate shadows and glare and can be used to highlight activity areas or decorative items. Recessed lighting is available in a variety of styles to provide general illumination from above. Chandeliers are popular options for

dining room lighting. Hang them about 30 inches above the table in a room with an 8-foot ceiling; for each additional foot of ceiling height, raise the fixture 3 inches.

If you include floor lamps in your lighting plan, provide the best light by selecting models that are 40 to 49 inches from the floor to the bottom of the shade. Torchères placed in corners supply beautiful accent lighting. Plan plenty of electrical outlets so you can rearrange your rooms and always be able to place lamps close to an outlet. This minimizes the risk that someone will trip over the cords.

For table lamps, look for shades that direct light both upward and downward. For reading, the bottom of the shade should be just below eye level.

It's important to provide quality lighting in areas where reading and other specialized tasks occur. Here, undercabinet fixtures provide focused illumination for the desk area.

Photo courtesy of Progress Lighting

An overall lighting plan might include recessed canisters for general or ambient light.

Also consider subtle wall-washers, sconces, rope lighting, and other decorative options to enhance your living spaces. Illuminating cabinets, bookshelves, artwork, and display cases with interior lighting can produce an elegant effect.

Easy Lighting

Make lighting easy to use by providing access to light switches at the entrance to the room. Light switches placed 40 to 44 inches above the floor are comfortable for people who are standing, as well as those who use wheelchairs. Rocker switches are easiest to turn on and off. Consider adding dimmers for overhead lights to adjust your light level to your mood or activity. Or have automated sensors installed, which turn on and off when people enter or leave a room. Select lamps with switches rather than pull chains and knobs, which are harder for people with less hand strength to operate. Lamp bases that turn on when you touch them are even easier.

Bulb Choices

Household bulbs are rated for indoor or outdoor use or both. Select bulbs that offer the amount, quality, and color of light you desire and that best fit the fixtures in your home. The most common bulbs are:

Incandescent. Providing white light, these bulbs vary in energy efficiency and hours of life. They operate on 12 or 24 volts.

Fluorescent. Fluorescent tubes last longer than incandescent bulbs and come in a wide spectrum of colors. To slash energy costs, try **compact fluorescents (CFLs)**. They'll work in most fixtures, but perform best in open fixtures that allow airflow.

Halogen. For bright, white lighting, try quartz halogen lights. They are usually low-voltage and emit minimal heat. Use with fixtures designed specifically for halogen lights.

LED (light emitting diodes). Formerly used on digital clocks and Christmas lights, LEDs are now available for use in indoor fixtures, too. Emitting illumination similar to natural sunlight, these energy-saving bulbs last 100 times longer than standard incandescents.

Safety Tip

Cleaning light fixtures and changing bulbs can be a difficult and even dangerous endeavor, particularly with overhead lighting. Minimize these chores by selecting easy-to-clean light fixtures with easily changed light bulbs. Also select long-lasting, energy-saving bulbs (such as CFLs) to minimize how often the bulbs must be changed.

Storage Solutions

Include plenty of storage in your living spaces to eliminate clutter and make finding things easier. Storing items where they belong eliminates tripping hazards—plus having a tidy home can improve your state of mind.

The first question to ask yourself is: What do I need to store? Let the answer lead you to the right storage components, with an eye toward options that put most-used items within easy reach of people who are sitting or standing.

Simple shelves provide streamlined storage and display (below). Include drawers underneath your window seat to maximize otherwise unused space (right). Storage cubes double as benches or a coffee table; soft, rounded edges mean bumping into them doesn't hurt (bottom right).

Photo courtesy of JELD-WEN Windows & Doors

Photo courtesy of Sherwin-Williams

Photo © James A. Stepp

This media center hides the television's cables and wires while providing storage and display space.

Open shelving is one of the most accessible storage options, whether you use stock units, build your own shelves, or remove the doors from cabinets already in your home.

Floor-to-ceiling bookshelves are ideal for a room in which you plan to display a large collection of books. In a family room, a built-in entertainment center or freestanding armoire that includes shelves and drawers is perfect for keeping CDs, DVDs, and media equipment organized. For hobby areas, a combination of open and closed storage keeps supplies and equipment close at hand while hiding clutter. And in office spaces, look for lateral filing cabinets, drawers, and pull-out organizers that easily open and close to minimize reaching to access items stored at the back.

For hallway closets, consider installing an organization system with a combination of shelves and drawers to fit your storage needs.

A desk area surrounded by shelves and open cubbies makes it easy to find and grab items.

Cost Estimates

Flooring

If you're having a new floor installed, consider a smooth surface material and eliminate or minimize thresholds. This reduces tripping hazards and makes it easier to roll anything—from a wheelchair to a kitchen cart to a stroller—around the house. Seven different flooring materials—and their costs per square foot—are listed in the box below, along with costs for carpet padding and new underlayment (particleboard beneath finished flooring). Note that the costs are based on sufficient quantities of work. (Small rooms or areas may have a higher price per square foot.) New underlayment may not be needed if the existing material is in good shape.

Flooring Options

Costs per Square Foot Installed	
Pre-finished oak strip flooring	$10.70
Laminate flooring	$9.00
Sheet vinyl flooring	$8.25
Vinyl tiles	$6.05
Ceramic tile flooring	$12.95
Cork tile flooring	$10.00
Carpeting (per square yard)	$57.00
Carpet pad (per square yard)	$6.50
$^{3}/_{8}"$ Particleboard underlayment	$2.25

Other Cost Factors:

- Removing old ceramic or stone tile can be more involved and add to the cost.

- Old vinyl flooring may contain asbestos and could require a certified professional to test and remove it.

- New wood and vinyl flooring can, in some cases, be installed over an existing, un-embossed vinyl or linoleum floor in good condition.

Photo courtesy of Quick-Step Inc.

Oak flooring makes a stunning statement in this spacious dining room. Keep floors free of rugs to minimize the risk that someone might trip or slip when traveling through the room.

Raised Fireplace

Installing a fireplace is generally a good investment in terms of adding to a home's ambience, comfort, and sales appeal. Selecting an efficient model and placing it at an accessible level only adds to its value. The estimate below includes costs for framing, rough-in gas piping, and electrical wiring for a prefabricated fireplace and vents. All costs include contractor's labor and overhead and are based on national averages.

Estimate Breakdown

Raised gas fireplace to include all framing, gypsum wallboard, trim, and prefabricated firebox. Firebox allowance: $1750.00	$3,200.00
Gas fitting	$350.00
Electrical connection	$250.00
Sub-total	**$3,800.00**
	(Add local sales tax for total)

This gas fireplace model works with a remote control or a wall thermostat.

Photo courtesy of Travis Industries

6

Bedrooms

Bedrooms should be havens designed to stand apart from the rest of the home. The master bedroom is a private retreat for preparing for the day, winding down in the evening, and getting a good night's rest. Start with a comfortable bed and smartly arranged furnishings, then add soft fabrics and the right combination of color and lighting to complete the space.

Floor Plan Basics

Allowing enough space for sleeping quarters should be a priority as you create your universally designed home. A spacious bedroom allows you to arrange furnishings in a way that makes it easy to get around—day or night.

Bedrooms should ideally be on the main floor for easy access. If your home has two or more stories, locate at least the master bedroom and bath on the first floor so it can be reached without climbing stairs. If you're happy with the master suite on an upper floor now, consider the future—perhaps by identifying an area on the main floor that could be converted to a master suite should the need arise. A spacious home office and adjacent sitting room backing up to a powder room for plumbing access might be good candidates for future conversion to a main level master suite. Another option might be building a first-floor master suite as an addition to your home.

Master Bedrooms

A master bedroom should be a quiet, welcoming sanctuary for relaxing and sleeping. If you are building a new home, consider positioning your master suite at the back of the house so your sleep won't be interrupted by street noise or bright lights.

Ideally, the master bedroom will include its own adjoining bathroom; but at the least, locate an easily accessible bathroom nearby. As you furnish and decorate the bedroom, keep the path from the bedroom to the bath clear of obstacles so traveling between the two—especially at night—is safe and easy.

Multifunctional Spaces

The most restful bedroom environment is one that is used for little else besides sleeping and relaxing. Yet many bedrooms need to serve other functions as well. Consider how to accommodate these other needs without disrupting your sleep.

First, take stock of what else will occur in the bedroom—dressing for the day, watching television, exercising, or working from home are all possibilities. Try to separate these areas from the bed, and look for ways to minimize their impact on your sleeping space. An

Photo used with permission of Inter IKEA Systems B.V.

A private bathroom located in the bedroom suite makes it easier to navigate between the two night or day. Pocket doors allow for privacy without taking up the floor space that standard hinged doors occupy.

Photo courtesy of Armstrong World Industries, Inc.

Soothing colors, plenty of daytime light, and ample floor space around the bed make this sleeping area restful and easy to navigate.

attractive screen is one way to block views of a desk or workout equipment. Hide the television behind the doors of a striking armoire when it's not in use.

Guest Suite or Apartment

It is becoming increasingly common for homes to include a guest suite. Similar to a master suite, these spaces often include a bedroom with an adjacent bathroom. Some even have their own kitchenettes and laundry areas to provide guests with private living quarters separate from your family's daily life.

Comfort, safety, and privacy are important components of any guest suite. If this area is likely to be used by someone who is older or has a condition that affects mobility or the senses, your first priority should be to implement necessary universal design recommendations (particularly for the kitchen and bath areas). If the guest suite is to be located in the basement, you may need to include an elevator, stairlift, or lower-level walkout entrance in your plan.

Communication Devices

Different types of communication devices in your home help you stay in contact with friends and relatives, easily communicate with family members within your home, and summon help should the need arise. Some things to consider:

Telephones. For easy access, include telephone jacks in all major living areas, including your kitchen, living/family room, and bedroom. This ensures that you can easily answer a call without having to rush to the next room. Portable phones are another option, although they're relatively easy to misplace and must be charged regularly. Telephones with lighted keypads and large buttons are best; look for models that have speed dial, too, so emergency services or family members can be reached with the touch of a single button. A speakerphone option allows you to speak on the phone without having to hold the handset. Also look for telephones with lights that flash when the phone rings if someone in your home has some hearing loss.

Intercom systems. Being able to communicate with family members in other parts of the house is helpful—especially if you live in a large home with multiple floors. You can have intercom systems installed in your home when it's built or remodeled, or purchase a portable wireless intercom system.

Emergency options. It's relatively easy to set up a personal emergency response system (PERS) using purchased or rented equipment from national manufacturers, local distributors, or hospitals. A PERS is a small, battery-powered radio transmitter that can be worn on a necklace or wristband or carried in a pocket. Should an emergency arise, you push the button on the transmitter and it sends a radio signal to a console that automatically dials one or more pre-selected emergency telephone numbers—contacting an emergency response center or a list of family members and neighbors.

Fabrics & Furnishings

A comfortable bed that provides a good night's sleep is the most important furnishing in a bedroom. Look for rounded corners and edges on all furniture and soft, durable fabrics.

While the basics in a bedroom include the bed, nightstands, and bureaus, your space might also include a seating area, TV, and bookshelves. Fabrics are an important component in a relaxing bedroom—whether in the form of bedding, window treatments, or furniture upholstery, they can add a touch of luxury to your space.

Furniture

Choose a sturdy, comfortable bed. The most important choice you'll make is the mattress. (For buying tips, see the sidebar on page 105.) Look for a durable, well-made box spring and bed frame, and avoid sharp corners. The ideal bed height allows your feet to touch the floor when you are seated on the side of the bed. A frame that places the mattress at the same height as the seat of a wheelchair (approximately 18 inches) makes it easier for a person who uses one to get in and out of bed; adjustable handrails that attach to the bed frame are also helpful. For people who have circulation or other health issues that require keeping their upper body or legs elevated in bed, an adjustable electric bed is a smart option. It also adds convenience if you like to prop up while reading in bed.

Include a bedside table with a wall or table lamp on each side of the bed if two people share the room. If there isn't enough space on both sides, consider "floating" nightstands, affixed directly to the wall with no legs to take up space below. This lends a contemporary look to your bedroom and also allows people who use wheelchairs to get closer to the table and bed. (Just make certain floating nightstands are securely affixed to wall studs.)

In considering storage options (closets, dressers, bureaus, trunks, armoires, and bookshelves), match your choices to the needs of each person. In a shared bedroom, you may wish to allow separate storage for each occupant. (Learn more about storage options on pages 112–113.)

If your bedroom is large enough, consider including a seating area for reading and relaxing. Select a comfortable chair or loveseat

Photo used with permission of Inter IKEA Systems B.V.

Sturdy furnishings and washable fabrics fill this welcoming nursery. Including a full-sized bed in the room provides a spot for tired parents to rest or for guests. When baby outgrows it, the crib can be removed while the rest of the furnishings stay.

Photo courtesy of VELUX America Inc.

A nightstand flanked by twin-size beds is a practical setup for kids' rooms. The light switch on the wall allows children to climb into bed before turning off the light.

with solid arms and a firm seat, and include a small table with a reading lamp. For more comfort, purchase an ottoman for putting your feet up.

Keep in mind when buying furniture: individual pieces sometimes take up less space than a matched set. Buying individual pieces also

Safety Tip

Safety is particularly important in children's rooms. This includes making certain all rugs have nonskid backing, child-proofing electrical outlets, and avoiding or at least securing drapery, blinds, and cords so they're out of reach. Keep breakable items and small accessories out of the way, too. Near cribs this includes making sure mobiles and other hanging toys are suspended out of baby's reach. In addition, place your child's bed away from windows or use window guards for safety. And affix shelves, bookcases, and other heavy furnishings to the wall so they don't topple on top of kids who might lean or try to climb on them.

Furnishing Kids' Rooms

Children's bedrooms will change over time—from crib and changing table to furnishings that will take them through adolescence.

To get the most from the furniture you purchase, look for sturdy, classic items that you can continue to use—either in your child's room or elsewhere in the home—over time. Here are some other suggestions when it comes to universal design:

Beds. Purchase a stable, quality bed or crib that meets national safety standards and has a firm, tight-fitting mattress. For babies, look for an adjustable-height crib, which can be raised and lowered to reduce the strain of leaning and lifting a child.

Seating. Include task areas, such as a cozy chair upholstered in durable fabric for reading. You may wish to include pint-size seating for toddlers as well.

Work areas. In a baby's room, include a waist-height changing table or surface outfitted with a changing pad, and keep frequently used items nearby minimize bending and reaching. For young children, a small table and chairs can provide a spot for coloring and other activities. Older kids will benefit from an out-of-the-way desk with a comfortable chair. Plan for plenty of lighting, such as task and overhead lighting and long-lasting LED lights.

Storage. Beyond a dresser and closet, include open shelves for easy access to books and toys. Stashing toys in lightweight drawers, bins, or baskets on low shelves encourages children to put their toys away and is a safer option than tossing items into a heavy toy chest with a lid that could pinch fingers. Include low hooks for hanging items within reach.

allows you to select the exact size and style you want for a particular spot—plus you can have fun creating a more interesting bedroom that fits your personal style.

Furniture Arranging

Because the bed typically is the focal point of the room, determine its location first. Consider the possible views to the outdoors, natural light, and indoor views, such as television. If you're building a new home or installing new windows, have them positioned with the sill no higher than 30 inches above the floor for optimum viewing.

In a bedroom shared by two people, allow for an unobstructed aisle at least 36 inches wide on each side and at the foot of the bed. To provide wheelchair turnaround space, include an open area 60 inches in diameter on one side of the bed if possible. Once you have allotted clear floor space for getting in and out of bed and traveling from the bed to the bathroom, you can begin arranging the other furnishings. Positioning dressers and other large items against the wall helps maximize floor space, but seating areas can be placed away from the wall if there is room, as long as they're out of the way of the flow of traffic.

Fabrics

As the focal point of most bedrooms, the bed should feature attractive, comfortable bedding. Look for fabrics that are soft (like high-thread-count cotton) but not slippery (like silk or satin) for sheets, layer on light-weight blankets as needed, then top the bed with an attractive comforter or duvet. To make wash day easy, use a duvet cover that's simple to remove. For allergy sufferers, consider adding dust mite-proof mattress and pillow covers. Although decorative pillows add a personality to the bedroom, limiting them makes it easier to make the bed each day and cuts down on dust accumulation.

A few well-placed fabric patterns can enhance the appearance of a bedroom, but too many vibrant prints can be visually jarring in a room that should be peaceful and relaxing. One design trick is to choose a dominant neutral fabric for the comforter and the curtains, then to bring in complementary colors and patterns for pillows, upholstered chairs, and other smaller items. Another way to bring fabric into the bedroom is to create a cushioned headboard covered in a textured material; as an added bonus, this provides more safety and comfort than a hard headboard.

In a smaller bedroom, a headboard that combines the functionality of a nightstand with additional storage frees up space around the bed. Wall-mount lights provide task lighting; just make certain the controls are easy to reach.

The dark wood and white upholstery of this room's furnishings balance a high-impact red accent wall. The contrast makes it easier for someone with vision loss to identify room features.

Photo courtesy of Armstrong World Industries, Inc.

Mattress Selection

As you shop for a mattress, look for a model that best fits your sleep habits and age—what is comfortable for a 25-year-old might not be the best option for a 75-year-old.

If you have back, neck, or shoulder pain, your bed may be the culprit. Let your salesperson know so he or she can help you select the best mattress for your needs. Test a variety of styles at the store; go ahead and lie down for a while so you can be certain the mattress is comfortable.

As you try out mattresses in the store, take note of which features are most comfortable for you. To ensure durability, purchase the highest-quality sleep set you can afford.

One of the most important mattress considerations is support. Look for a mattress that keeps your spine in alignment and gently supports your body—particularly your shoulders, hips, and lower back.

Commonly used innerspring mattresses have coils inside for support. For the most comfort, look for a mattress with tightly packed coils; zone-specific coils may help provide additional support to areas that need it most, such as the lower back. Memory foam mattresses are a popular option at hospitals and rehabilitation centers because they keep your body's pressure evenly distributed over the entire surface of the mattress, which can help reduce aches and back pain. For people who spend a considerable amount of time in bed, a quality, low-pressure air mattress is another possibility because it produces less pressure on the body than innerspring mattresses and has been shown to reduce the risk of bedsores.

Some people prefer cushiony pillow top mattresses, but they won't provide as much support as other models because the pillow top masks the firmness of the mattress below it. If you prefer a pillow top mattress, look for a double-sided model that can be flipped, which doubles the mattress life.

Some mattresses are available with specialized functions, such as heat and massage. If you share a bed, mattresses that allow you to adjust the firmness of each side may be useful, but make certain the uneven firmness of the bed doesn't cause the person on the firmer side to roll to the softer side.

To provide additional relief, you may wish to purchase a mattress overlay pad. Look for memory foam, egg crate foam, or air mattress pads. Orthopedic neck pillows that support your spine's natural curve and back pillows that minimize pressure on your lower back also may help you get a good night's rest.

Flooring

Select durable bedroom flooring that is comfortable whether you're wearing shoes or barefoot. Eliminate tripping hazards to ensure a safe walk between the bedroom and bath.

Depending on your tastes, carpet, hardwood, or cork are popular choices for bedroom floors. In hot climates, nonslip tile (which is cool underfoot) is another option.

Tightly woven, low-pile carpet provides durability and is comfortable to walk on without shoes. This type of carpeting also tends to wear well, which is important in areas where the same traffic patterns are used day after day.

Should you choose hardwood flooring for your bedroom, you may wish to place nonskid rugs for warmth. (But take care to keep rugs out of

Photo courtesy of Armstrong World Industries, Inc.

main traffic pathways—they can become a tripping hazard, particularly if someone is using a walker or trying to reach the bathroom in the middle of the night.) Keep in mind that if you or another member of your household frequently wears high heels or if you have a dog, wood may not be the best option as heels or claws may damage the floor.

Cork is a popular alternative because it is warm, soft underfoot, and durable, plus it's a good option for people who suffer from allergies because it is an all-natural material.

A number of hardwood flooring options are available for use in homes. This distinct grain pattern disguises nicks and scratches better than a clearer-grained variety, helping the floor look good longer.

The wall treatment in your bedroom greatly affects the style and feel of the space. Contemplate what mood you want to create before you select a wall color or covering.

Wall Treatments

Paint, wallpaper, and even fabric are great starting points for bedroom walls. Up the style even more with architectural details such as crown molding, wall paneling, or wainscoting.

Wallpaper—particularly if it's textured—can help absorb some sound, which may make your sleeping spaces a bit quieter. Keep in mind, however, that large-scale, all-over prints can make a bedroom seem smaller. If you choose patterned wallpaper, minimize patterns elsewhere in the room for a more relaxing effect.

Covering walls in fabric is another option that helps create a quiet, romantic retreat. Fabrics often have colors, patterns, and textures that wallpaper and paint can't duplicate; plus some types of fabric help block sound. The easiest way to upholster walls is by stapling fabric to the walls and ceilings, then covering the staples with millwork. Fabric-covered walls can be cleaned with a vacuum attachment, much as you care for window treatments.

Of course, you can't go wrong with paint. In a bedroom, where traffic and messes are limited, flat paint works well and helps hide surface imperfections. Plus matte-finish paints are better for people with limited vision; walls that are too glossy may create glare. For a more striking effect, consider applying subtle decorative paint treatments. Insulating paint is another option worth considering, because it prevents heat from escaping through the outside walls, improving the comfort of your bedroom and reducing energy costs.

Photo courtesy of Thibaut

The hue of this subtly patterned wallpaper inspired the color scheme for this tranquil room.

Color

Color choices are very personal, whether you prefer warm and welcoming or cool and serene. Choose a bedroom wall color that exudes harmony and comfort, and you'll want to spend more time in your special haven.

The basics of color (see pages 90–91) apply to every room in the home. Yet the colors you choose for the bedroom should help you navigate safely in low light and create a calm atmosphere ideal for sleep and relaxation.

Quiet, muted colors help create a soothing environment and are usually easiest on the eye. But it's important to choose colors that you love and that make you comfortable, so feel free to select deep jewel tones or cheerful hues if you prefer them over neutral colors.

Color Techniques

A number of options may guide color choices in your bedroom. For instance, if you're a morning person who spends quite a bit of time in your bedroom when you first awake, you may want energetic colors on your walls. Do you like to relax in your sleeping spaces in the evening before bed? Cooler hues may be for you. For subtle visual interest, paint tone-on-tone stripes, such as shades of brown, taupe, cream, or white on the wall.

To ensure furnishings and other items in your room stand out against the walls and make it easy to see in low light or with reduced vision, use paint or wallpaper in colors that contrast with the hues of your furnishings and fabrics.

Because much of the time spent in the bedroom involves lying down, consider the color of your ceiling as well. Adding a subtle tint of the wall color to the ceiling paint can help create continuity and serenity.

Color choices aren't reserved for the walls and ceiling. In fact, you may wish to use neutral walls as a backdrop and play with color elsewhere in the room. Fabrics, rugs, artwork, and accessories provide opportunities for adding color without overwhelming your bedroom. This also allows you to change accents or create an entirely new color scheme when the season changes or the mood strikes.

Photo courtesy of Dunn-Edwards Corporation

Pairing a dark headboard, table, and lamp shade with cool blue walls ensures that a person with some vision loss can distinguish elements in this bedroom.

Serene green creates a calming backdrop for this subdued master bedroom filled with colors and patterns inspired by nature.

Warm, dark hues make rooms seem cozier and more intimate. The shag rug provides subtle color now, but can easily be removed or changed for low-pile carpet later.

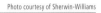

Soothing Hues

A bedroom decorated in calming colors can make relaxing and sleeping easier. But soothing doesn't have to mean boring—and it doesn't require limiting your color choices either. Consider these options:

Cool hues such as greens, blues, and lavenders are calming and can lead to feelings of peacefulness and tranquility, making them the perfect choice for bedrooms. Another benefit of painting with cool colors: they visually recede, which helps makes a room appear larger than it is.

Warm colors don't have to be bold and energetic—some shades work just as well in serene settings. Opt for soft hues, such as buttery yellows, subtle peaches, or delicate pinks.

Neutral shades such as beige and cream naturally lend themselves to calm, understated, yet elegant spaces. They create the perfect backdrop for playing with fabric and other accents.

Lighting

A combination of natural and artificial lighting is important in bedrooms for function and mood. Remember to include proper illumination for safety at night.

The best bedroom lighting includes multiple sources, including natural light from windows, overhead lighting, and focused lighting near the bed, in the closet, and at any other task areas. Including a consistent level of light between the hallway and bedroom makes moving between these spaces easier on the eyes.

For overhead lighting, a combination ceiling fan and light is a good choice. Dimmer switches can soften the intensity of overhead lights. Allow for plenty of electrical outlets in the bedroom, mounted 18 to 30 inches above the floor rather than at baseboard level to make them easier to reach. To eliminate glare, look for lamps with opaque, light-colored shades.

Light Controls

Many of today's lighting options offer easy-to-use controls. Consider three-way fixtures that allow you to change the light level by touching the base of the lamp. Lighting that turns on automatically when you enter a room or open closet doors eliminates the need to reach for switches or pulls. And photosensitive nightlights that turn off or on depending on the light levels in your room enable you to easily find your way into the bathroom at night. Nightlights should offer safety, but be subtle enough that they don't interfere with sound sleep.

Windows

Regardless of where they are located in the house, windows should be secure, well-insulated, and easy to operate. At least one window in each room should be operable. Windows providing an opening of at least 30 inches are generally wide enough to permit a person to pass through in an emergency. Because wheelchair seat height is generally 18 inches, window sills located no higher than 24 inches above the floor will allow someone using a wheelchair to transfer onto the window sill or be easily lifted up onto the sill and then helped out through the windows.

Opening and closing windows can be difficult for people with limited strength, particularly

Photo © Jupiterimages

An oval window centered above the headboard allows daylight into this master bedroom and contributes to the elegance of the room. At night, lamps on the bedside tables provide task lighting.

Quality lighting is important in walk-in closets so you can see clearly when selecting clothes and dressing. Look for light bulbs with a CRI (color rendering index) of 90 or higher for truest color.

if they require sliding or lifting the sash. For this reason, casement windows are a good choice—they easily open and close by turning a hand crank and can be operated while users are seated or standing. Instead of replacing double-hung or sliding windows that are in good shape, you can have your current windows retrofitted to include a crank and latch.

When purchasing new windows, look for energy-efficient models with low-E coating and double- or triple-pane glass.

Some of the easiest ways to control light and reduce glare from windows are, of course, blinds, shades, and curtains. If you prefer a full view, installing window film can help minimize glare and reduce fading of furnishings.

Lighting at Night

Bedrooms require different light qualities during the day than they do at night. "You want brightness during the day and very low light levels that are more amber and red at night," says Eunice Noell-Waggoner, L.C., President of the Center of Design for an Aging Society. It has to do with circadian rhythms—white, blue, or green light that shines in your bedroom in the night can wake you up and make it difficult to get back to sleep.

At night, block light by closing your bedroom door and hanging window treatments with blackout linings. For safety, include low-level automatic LED nightlights or another form of subtle illumination along the path to the bathroom.

Storage Solutions

In the bedroom, a smart combination of closet and freestanding storage ensures each item has a logical spot and remains within easy reach.

Bedroom storage options might include shelves, bureaus, armoires, trunks, bookcases, under-bed containers, and closets. Open shelving in closets is the easiest to use when it's positioned within an accessible reach range and is no more than 18 inches deep. There are no doors or drawers to open and close, and everything is visible. Boxes, totes, and baskets can help corral smaller objects on open shelving. If your storage includes drawers, make certain they are easy to open and close, for example with D-shaped handles or magnetic latches.

Photo courtesy of ClosetMaid.com

Closets

Walk-in closets provide the greatest usability for everyone if they include a 5-foot turning area. To get the most from your closet space and to customize it for the primary user, consider including an adjustable organization system. This may include a number of components made to fit your needs, such as adjustable clothing rods, tie racks, open cubbies, drawers, shoes shelves, pull-out baskets, and even motorized carousel systems (a smaller version of those used by dry cleaners) that allow you to bring items you need to the front of the closet. Low-cost, do-it-yourself storage systems may be made of wire, while costlier wood options often are sturdier and more attractive.

For an even more accessible closet area, make certain the doorway to the closet has a 32-inch-clear width. You can use swing-away hinges to enlarge the door opening, install pocket doors, or if you keep a tidy closet, remove closet doors altogether. Store items that are worn frequently within easy reach of people who are seated.

Movable items, such as this pull-out belt rack, make it easier to organize and reach clothing and accessories stored in the closet.

This closet organizer system provides threshold-free access and is hung on the wall studs to reduce the need for reaching. (It also provides space for a person who uses a wheelchair to roll close to the items stored there.)

In a spacious closet area, a bench provides additional storage as well as a place to sit while dressing. The variety of storage organizers accommodate people of different heights with ease.

A closet system needn't be custom-made to function well. Two tiers of wire racks, shoe shelves, and drawers keep this walk-in closet tidy. Recessed lights and a solar tube skylight provide plenty of illumination.

Cost Estimates

New First-Floor Bedroom

A universally designed bedroom should ideally be on the first floor. If your home has two or more stories, and you can't convert a downstairs room, an addition may be the answer.

First-floor master suites have become popular in homes across the country. Additions should be in proportion and blend seamlessly with the style and finish materials of your home.

This estimate shows national-average costs to build a 20×24-foot addition with a full basement below. It includes a concrete foundation, lumber for framing and sheathing, insulation, roofing and flooring, electrical and heating, windows and doors, siding, and finish materials. Costs include contractor's labor and overhead. (To add a new bath, see the estimate on pages 74–75.) Below the estimate are costs for different roofing and siding materials.

Estimate Breakdown

20' x 24' bedroom addition to include foundation, framing, roofing, siding, two windows, one interior door, insulation, drywall, and interior finish work.	$40,000.00
Electrical work to include eight duplex outlets, two single-pole switches, and all associated wiring.	$1,000.00
Heating work to include baseboard heating elements and connection to existing furnace.	$1,500.00
Sub-total	**$42,500.00**

(Add local sales tax for project total)

Siding Options

Costs per Square Foot Installed	
Brick Veneer	$18.00
Stone Veneer	$22.00
Beveled Cedar Lap Siding	$8.00
Vertical Redwood Siding	$9.50
White Cedar Shingles	$6.25
Red Cedar Shingles	$7.75
Vinyl Clapboard Siding	$6.50
Vertical Vinyl Siding	$6.50

Roofing Options

Costs per Square Foot Installed	
Laminated Asphalt shingles	$3.15
Cedar shingles	$6.65
Clay tile	$9.20

A spacious first-floor bedroom with wide doorways provides comfort and convenience now and into the future.

7

Laundry, Garage & Utility Spaces

These hardworking spaces could be overlooked as you focus on incorporating universal design into your home's main living areas. But think about how much time you spend doing laundry or how often you pass through your garage or utility areas. All of these spaces will be safer, more accessible, and more attractive with universal design as part of the plan.

Laundry Spaces

Outfitting a laundry room involves more than purchasing a washer and dryer. Select durable, energy-efficient appliances, position them for ease of use, and factor in storage, seating, and space for folding clothes.

In many homes laundry spaces are hidden in the basement, which means you have to climb steep stairs while carrying laundry baskets or piles of clothes. This isn't safe for anyone and becomes particularly troublesome if you or someone in your family is no longer able to easily navigate stairs. To ensure this never becomes a problem, situate the laundry room in an accessible area on the main floor of your home. With a variety of washer and dryer sizes and styles (and quieter models than ever before), you can create laundry areas in a hallway closet, an out-of-the-way corner of the kitchen, the mudroom, or a bathroom.

Washers and Dryers

Front-loading washers and dryers are increasingly popular because they are more efficient, allow you to load and unload laundry while seated, and eliminate the need to reach down into the appliance to fish out clothing. Consider models with controls located on the front. To make machines even more accessible, you can purchase models with pedestals that raise them 12 to 15 inches above the floor. Look for the ENERGY STAR label for the most efficient models.

Keep in mind that your washer and dryer should each be on a separate, grounded circuit. A washer requires a drain and hot and cold water supply pipes. Gas dryers require gas supply lines. Dryers should be vented to the outside of your home.

Room Setup

The larger your laundry area, the more usable it will be. Plan for wide doorways and at least a 5-foot-diameter area of open floor space in front of the washer and dryer, if possible.

With front-loading washers and dryers, try to allow at least 48 inches of clearance in front of each machine so you have space to stand or sit and open the doors. This space will also allow

Many front-loading washer and dryer models come in attractive colors other than standard white. Pedestals may be purchased that raise the height of the appliances and provide additional storage for detergent.

A well-designed laundry room may include an elevated washer and dryer, a sink with knee space below, and a rolling laundry cart.

Keeping the laundry room tidy is easy with shelves, pull-out racks, and hampers for storing clothes, cleaning supplies, and more.

for pulling the machines out for repairs or replacement should the need arise.

Placing a table or countertop near the washer and dryer at a height of 28 to 30 inches allows you to sit and fold clothes. A fold-down shelf or rolling laundry cart is another option.

If you plan to include a laundry sink, it should ideally be no higher than 34 inches above the finished floor and include knee space below (that isn't obstructed by sink plumbing) for seated users. A rod above the sink is helpful for hanging items to drip-dry.

Cabinetry or open shelving provide storage for laundry and cleaning supplies. Include some storage within reach of seated users. Consider additional items such as bins for separating clothing, a foldable drying rack, and an adjustable-height clothing rod for hanging clean clothes to minimize wrinkling.

If there's room, an adjustable-height ironing board is handy for seated or standing users. A fold-out model conserves space.

This spacious laundry room includes a portable countertop for folding laundry, a sewing area, and pantry-style storage. The washer and dryer would be easier to use if they had front-mount controls.

Flooring and Lighting

It's important to include a floor drain in the laundry room to protect your home from water damage in case the washer leaks or a hose breaks. One option is to install the washer over a shower base with a floor drain; another is to construct the floor so that it slopes toward a drain in the center of the room. If you choose the latter option, it's best to protect the subfloor with a waterproof membrane.

Consider covering a cold concrete floor with durable, easy-clean finish flooring such as vinyl tile or laminate. Cork provides a level of

Photo courtesy of Progress Lighting

Flexible track lighting illuminates a multifunctional room that includes a washer and dryer, ample counterspace, and storage for sewing and craft supplies.

comfort when you are standing for tasks like ironing—and it's naturally water-resistant.

Motion-detector lighting is helpful for laundry rooms because people often enter and leave with their arms full. To minimize eye strain and fatigue, supplement overhead illumination with task lighting above laundry machines and workstations or wherever folding and ironing are done.

Laundry Locations

If you don't have a specific room in your home to devote to a washer and dryer, you might be able to create a laundry area in one of these spaces:

- **Hallway closet.** If large enough, this is a convenient location for laundry—particularly if it's near bedrooms. The closet should be sized to allow for additional floor space on either side of the appliances, and the closet doors should fold back against the wall for maximum usability.

- **Bathroom.** Compact stackable washer and dryer units with front-mounted controls allow more placement options—including a corner or closet in a bathroom. Placing the washer and dryer in a large shared bathroom minimizes the distance clothing must be hauled. Consider whether the noise would disrupt anyone trying to sleep in nearby bedrooms.

- **Butler's pantry.** A pantry or hallway near the kitchen is preferable to placing the washer and dryer right in the kitchen. Keep in mind the humidity, dust, vapors, and noise the machines produce. For these reasons, a door that can be closed is a plus.

- **Breezeway or mudroom.** These spaces are often located near the kitchen, too. A bonus: Messy kids can peel muddy sweatshirts, socks, and other items off right when they walk in the door rather than tracking through the house.

- **Shared spaces.** A craft room, exercise area, or other space may be large enough for a washer and dryer.

Are your bedrooms located on the second floor of your home, but the laundry room is on the first floor? Build a laundry chute so you don't have to haul dirty clothing downstairs.

Garage Setups

Sometimes there are so many other items stashed in the garage that the family car doesn't fit. A bit of planning ensures everything is easy to access—including your vehicle.

Keeping your garage clutter-free and well-lit makes it easy to get from the car to the house, create a workshop area, and store items out of the way but within reach. The key is to leave plenty of room for the main occupants of the space (your vehicles) and to place all other items in logical, organized spots.

If you're building or remodeling a garage, make it big enough to accommodate SUVs or trucks if you have the space.

Access

Single-bay garage doors are usually 9 feet wide and 7 to 8 feet high. Plan on 8 feet high for a large SUV or pickup truck, higher for special vehicles. An automatic garage door opener makes life easier, and an electric sensor prevents the door from closing on people or objects. An easy-to-reach push-button keypad outside the garage allows you access without keys or your car opener. Look for keypads with large, lighted buttons.

A variety of garage door designs are available, allowing you to find one that best fits the style and color of your house. Doors with windows allow a level of light into the garage.

Photo courtesy of JELD-WEN Windows & Doors

The larger your garage, the easier it will be to access your vehicle and stored items. Open space around a parked car gives you room to assist small children or people who use wheelchairs, while still allowing ample space for storing tools and sports and yard equipment. If possible, include an aisle at least 5 feet wide adjacent to the vehicle; lift-equipped vehicles may require an 8-foot aisle. If you have a two-car garage, parking only one vehicle in it provides this space.

If your garage is not directly attached to your home, consider building a sheltered breezeway to connect them.

Like exterior doors found elsewhere in the home, the door from the garage to the house should be wide—with lever-style handles and secure, easy-to-maneuver locks. Automatic door openers can be installed on house doors to

open them with the push of a button, which is helpful for people who are carrying packages, wheeling a stroller or luggage, or using a walker or wheelchair.

Building codes often require a step or curb between the house and the garage floor to prevent spilled gasoline and carbon monoxide fumes from entering the house. (If these codes do not apply in your area, thresholds should not be higher than ¼ inch.) Codes typically require a garage floor to slope from front to back; check local codes for specific requirements.

If there are steps leading from the garage to the house, add a railing on both sides 34 to 38 inches high that can support at least 250 pounds. A second, lower handrail 28 inches high is helpful for people of short stature. It's smart to allot enough clear space near the steps in case it's necessary to build a ramp later.

Safety Tip

Proper ventilation is important in the garage, where you may store flammable items. Installing vents or an exhaust fan is a good idea if you spend a considerable amount of time working in the garage. Make certain the vent controls are easy to reach. If your garage has windows, ensure that they are functional and that the pathway to them is clear.

This deluxe garage includes a workshop with a variety of storage options: cabinets, drawers, and slat-walls for suspending frequently used tools.

Flooring

Most garages have concrete floors. For safety, repair cracks and clean up spills as soon as they appear. Concrete can be slick when wet. Nonslip coatings or sealers can be applied to increase slip-resistance. Materials such as textured vinyl or rubber are also used over concrete.

A rubber mat or piece of carpet, securely affixed to the floor, can help minimize fatigue and back strain if you plan to spend time standing at a workbench. Mats for wiping feet at the door to the house should also stay firmly in place, and should be thin, so they're less likely to cause tripping.

Lighting and Electricity

Automatic garage door openers often come with an overhead light that stays on for a certain amount of time after the garage door is opened or closed. Other helpful lighting features include motion-detector lights and lighted switches, so you don't have to find and flip a switch in the dark.

Choose CFL (compact fluorescent light) bulbs. You'll save energy and won't have to change

This stretch of countertop is perfect for potting plants. Durable, easy-open doors and drawers ensure your garage storage options will last.

Exterior lighting for the garage is almost as important as lighting its interior, so drivers can easily see where they're going at night.

them often. Regular fluorescent or halogen fixtures can also serve as task lighting.

If you're remodeling or building a new garage, allow plenty of electrical power, with enough well-placed outlets so that you can minimize the use of extension cords, which can be tripping hazards. GFCI receptacles will protect you from a shock if they are subjected to moisture. Position outlets at 18 inches above the floor along open walls to reduce the need for reaching and bending, and at workbench height in that area.

Garage Organization

Keeping your garage tidy is important for safety (not to mention your sanity). Garage organization systems from home centers and specialty storage companies can be simple or complex and vary widely in price. Stain-resistant laminate or plastic finishes, stainless steel, or hardwood treated to withstand humidity and solvents are durable material options for vertical surfaces. Here are some ways to keep everything in place:

- Divide the garage into zones by function. This might include special areas for gardening and lawn care, recycling, automotive, home improvement, general hardware, and sports and recreation. Position main work areas away from cars to limit disruptions and accidental damage.

- Use open storage as much as possible. Store tubs containing sports equipment and other items on sturdy, open shelves with the heaviest items on the lower shelves. Pegboard on the wall is handy for hanging small tools. Heavy-duty hooks work well for suspending garden equipment, bikes, and ladders.

- Include rolling storage so supplies are easy to reach.

- Provide at least 5 feet of clear space in front of work areas if possible.

- Keep floors clear with wall-hung workbenches and cabinets. Position at least one workbench no higher than 32 inches, with leg room at least 36 inches wide underneath, so people with back or leg problems can sit while working. Choose a sturdy countertop material, such as wood, for your workbench.

- Choose magnetic touch latches and C- or D-shaped handles so doors are easy to open.

- Avoid storing items overhead. Although ceiling-mount shelves allow you take advantage of space that would otherwise be wasted, accessing these items can be dangerous unless you have an electric storage lift or sturdy pulley system in place.

Utility Rooms

The mechanical equipment that keeps your home running is often relegated to the most cramped, inaccessible places in the house. If you're building or remodeling, plan utility placement to ensure you can easily reach these systems when needed.

It makes sense to centralize the location of utilities in your home to minimize the amount of ductwork and plumbing required. In many homes, this means that furnaces, water heaters, water softeners, and other mechanical equipment are crammed into a small area in the basement—not the most ideal spot. If you are planning a new home, consider the benefits of locating these items in a utility area on the main floor. Creating a mechanical and storage room near the garage or off a mudroom or breezeway ensures easy access. Or, if your utilities are located in the basement, place them in their own room or allow plenty of space around them in a shared room.

Access

Whether in its own room or in shared storage or laundry space, keep the path to each piece of equipment clear and uncluttered. Plan for doorways wide enough to move the largest piece of equipment in and out, and provide access for people who use wheelchairs. Position light switches within easy reach at the entrance of each room; a height of 40 to 44 inches from the floor is recommended.

Refer to user's manuals for each piece of equipment or contact manufacturers to ensure you provide enough space above and around the housing for air to circulate. Ideally, the utility area will include ample workspace (at least 30 inches wide by 30 inches high) around all appliances, especially the furnace control panel.

Systems

In addition to heating, cooling, and plumbing, whole-house vacuums, dehumidifiers, and water purifiers and softeners may also be installed in utility rooms. It's important to understand the basics of these systems and know what to do

When a utility area such as this one is located in the basement, it's best to section off the utilities in their own room. That way it's easy to keep the area free of clutter; plenty of open floor space ensures access to the equipment.

should problems arise. All adults in the house should familiarize themselves with the water and furnace shut-offs, hot water heater, and circuit breaker or fuse boxes.

Water passes into the house through a main shut-off valve, which is usually located in the basement or on an outside wall near the utility area of the house. When the valve is open, it allows full flow of water through the pipes; turning it off stops the water supply to the entire house. Find this valve and make certain you can shut it off (turn the handle clockwise to fully close the valve) so you won't have to scramble to figure out what to do should a plumbing problem, such as a burst pipe, occur. A problem related to a specific fixture or part of the house may not require shutting off the water to your entire home, so it's also important to identify shut-off valves located below or near immediate sources of water (such as the valve located directly below the toilet tank).

Most people don't even think about hot water heaters until the shower water runs cold, but maintaining your water heater once a year by flushing it out and testing the pressure-relief valve helps keep it in good working condition. Lowering the thermostat temperature may help prevent heat damage to the tank, saves energy,

and ensures that the water won't scald users. All water heaters have access panels; make sure yours is easy to reach in case worn-out parts need to be replaced.

A service panel, sometimes called a breaker or fuse box, is where you will shut off electricity to various circuits in your home should a problem arise or if electrical work is being done. When possible, install the service panel with the highest operable control no more than 50 inches above the floor with a 60×60 clear floor space in front.

Heating and Cooling

To keep your living spaces comfortable, consider the following:

- Thermostats, used to control the temperature in individual rooms or areas of the home, are easiest to use when they are illuminated and have large, readable, high-contrast letters and numbers. Thermostats should be no higher than 48 inches above the floor so people can adjust them while sitting or standing.

- Ceiling fans circulate cool air in the summer and (when switched to turn blades in the opposite direction) drive warm air down from the ceiling in the winter, helping to cut home energy costs and improve comfort. Look for ceiling fan models that come with a remote so you don't have to reach for a hanging cord to control them.

- Fireplaces add ambience and warmth. Some of the options are direct-vent gas, ventless gas, wood-burning fireplaces, and wood-burning stoves. Gas fireplaces are easy to manage and require less maintenance. A raised hearth minimizes bending when maintaining or enjoying the fire. Regardless of the type of fireplace you choose, be sure to check with local building codes before purchasing and installing it.

Safety Tip

Enjoying your new or remodeled home is much easier when you have peace of mind. To ensure whole-house safety, install smoke and carbon monoxide detectors in each area of the house (especially near bedrooms) and change the batteries once a year. For further protection against carbon monoxide poisoning, have your heating system and other fuel-burning appliances serviced yearly. Keep fire extinguishers in easy-to-reach locations in the kitchen, garage, and utility area. And store flashlights throughout the home so they are easy to find in case the power goes out.

Cost Estimates

New Attached Single Garage

Direct access between the car and house is a comfort and convenience fitting with universal design. Garages are also considered a must by many homebuyers today, so they're usually a good investment in your home's value.

This estimate covers costs to build a modest one-car garage attached to the home with a concrete foundation and slab, an asphalt-shingled roof, one insulated window, a door to the house, a sectional wood garage door, and cedar siding. Costs include contractor's labor and overhead and are based on national averages. Your project's costs will vary based on local economic conditions and availability of contractors, as well as the size of your garage and your material selections.

Additional costs may be incurred for site preparation such as tree, stump, and rock removal as well as grading and fill if the site is sloped. You might want to include additional windows, piping for an outdoor faucet, additional electrical outlets, or a new driveway.

Estimate Breakdown

Attached single-car garage to include all footings, foundation, framing, roofing, siding, doors, and window.	$12,000.00
Electrical work to include seven new duplex outlets, two light fixtures, and two single pole switches.	$800.00
Sub-total	**$12,800.00**
(Add local sales tax for job total)	

Siding Options

Costs per Square Foot Installed	
Brick Veneer	$18.00
Stone Veneer	$22.00
Beveled Cedar Lap Siding	$8.00
Vertical Redwood Siding	$9.50
White Cedar Shingles	$6.25
Red Cedar Shingles	$7.75
Vinyl Clapboard Siding	$6.50
Vertical Vinyl Siding	$6.50

Roofing Options

Costs per Square Foot Installed	
Laminated Asphalt shingles	$3.15
Cedar shingles	$6.65
Clay tile	$9.20

Driveway Options

If you'd like to add a new driveway, you have several material options. Here are some examples of costs per square foot. Keep in mind the desirability of a smooth surface for universal design when making your selection.

Gravel	6" thick	$0.85
Asphalt	2½" thick	$1.45
Concrete	6" thick	$5.85
Crushed Stone	1" thick	$0.70
Brick	1½" thick	$11.00
Paving Stones	2" thick	$26.50

Photo © Jupiterimages

A garage adds a level of comfort and convenience to your home. A sloped driveway allows you to keep the garage floor level with the first floor of your home.

8

Outdoor Living

Universal design should be a major consideration in planning outdoor spaces to ensure full enjoyment of your home for years to come. With a bit of forethought, you can create a beautiful, accessible patio or deck that seamlessly connects with your home's interior, expanding your daytime and evening living space. Special features like a pool, spa, and gardens personalize and add pleasure to your home.

Access & Traffic Flow

Allow everyone who lives in or visits your home to enjoy the outdoor spaces you have created by making it easy to access your patio, deck, and pathways.

As you plan the placement of your deck or patio, consider the best location for doors leading to it. If you want a quiet retreat for relaxing, you may wish to access your deck or patio from the master suite. For frequent entertaining, consider connecting to your family room. And if alfresco dining is your style, access from your kitchen makes it easy to bring food out and clean up after the meal is over.

Doors should be easy to open. Install a smooth-sliding patio door or wide double French doors with lever-style handles. A threshold that is flush (or not higher than ¼ inch) with the deck or patio eliminates the risk of tripping and makes it safer and easier to move in and out. A minimal threshold works for wheelchair users and also enables you to roll a cart of drinks, plates, or food in and out.

To prevent water from entering the home's interior (which can be a problem with a low threshold), allow for drainage by leaving a gap no less than ⅜ inch where the decking meets the door, installing drains within each threshold to divert water, and grading the patio away from the home with at least a 2 percent slope for run-off.

Also take into account traffic patterns on your deck or patio. Arrange furniture, potted plants, and other items out of the way of doors and away from paths to the backyard. Following some of the standard universal design guidelines for interior spaces can help: Include at least 5 feet of unobstructed turnaround space on your deck or patio, and allow for a minimum of 36 inches of clearance to accommodate passage around and through groupings of furniture.

Photo © Andersen Corporation

Sliding glass doors capitalize on views of outdoor spaces. Doors that easily slide open make traveling from the kitchen to the grill with platefuls of food less of a challenge.

To increase the enjoyment of your outdoor living areas, include gentle transitions and smooth pathways so it's easy to move from your deck or patio to the spaces beyond.

Transitions & Pathways

When you create transitions between your outdoor spaces, plan for stairs and ramps that are easy to travel up or down and smooth, wide pathways. To further enhance your outdoor spaces, include attractive, low-maintenance landscaping and elements like trellises or arbors that mark the edges of your deck or patio, provide shade, and reduce glare.

Easy Transitions

Being able to move easily from your deck or patio to the yard is important for safety—plus smooth transitions enhance the appearance of your outdoor spaces. Because patios are built directly on the ground, it should be easy to step from them into the rest of the yard. Unless they are low platform versions, decks are more of a challenge because they require stairs or ramps. (Learn about deck stairs and ramps on page 137. For general information about stairs and ramps, see pages 24–25.)

Pathways

Include pathways to provide access to key features of your yard and to facilitate movement around your house and to the garage, shed, and other structures. Plan walkways that are at least 3 feet wide; a path that's 48 to 54 inches wide is even better because it allows two people to walk on the path side by side.

Avoid gravel and other loose materials that can be difficult to walk on or roll over, as well as materials such as smooth stone, which may be slippery when wet. Lightly textured, even surfaces are best. Slightly tilting the

If you have long paths that meander through a large backyard or garden, place an attractive, sturdy bench with armrests along the way as a resting point.

Photo courtesy of Gloster Furniture Limited

walkway to one side or the other (called a "sloped wash") prevents water from settling into puddles—but avoid cross slopes steeper than 1:50. Poured concrete, asphalt, and pavers that lie flush with the ground make good pathways. You can also design attractive walkways using patio materials, such as decomposed granite sprayed with polymer to create a smooth, hard surface. Or, for the appearance of loose materials without the tripping hazard, pebbles can be set in concrete or acrylic polymer. Pathways may be used with decks, too—for example, a wooden walkway connecting separate areas of a large deck.

Walkway maintenance is important. Minimize hazards by repairing cracks and removing weeds. Colorful flowers, shrubs, or groundcover are great ways to visually distinguish the edges of a walkway, but steer clear of thorny or fast-growing plants that intrude into the path.

Shade

Creating shaded outdoor areas keeps people comfortable and protects those with light and heat sensitivity on a hot day. Shade options include trees, awnings, overhead structures, and umbrellas.

Because the amount of shade and sun your outdoor spaces receive will change throughout the day, position your deck or patio in an area that is shaded at the times you plan to use it most. For instance, space on the east side of the house will benefit from afternoon shade during the hottest months of the year. Spend time observing your yard at different seasons and times of the day to determine the best plan for adding shade when and where it's needed.

Sturdy table umbrellas offer shade for daytime dining. The white fabric reflects heat away from the seating area.

Photo courtesy of Gloster Furniture Limited

Trees

Building your deck or patio under or near mature trees provides natural shade and enhances the appearance of your outdoor spaces. Deciduous trees provide generous shade from hot summer sun when their leaves are full and allow more sun to reach the patio on cooler days in the spring and fall, when there are fewer leaves.

Shade Structures

If natural shade from trees isn't possible in your yard, you may wish to include structures that filter or block sunlight. An automated retractable awning can be extended when shade is needed or retracted when you prefer direct sunlight. Awnings also help cool the interior of your house in the summer.

Structures like a pergola or porch roof provide shade while adding architectural definition to a portion of your deck or patio. Both typically include support posts and rafters. Pergolas have an open roof built from lattice or narrow boards and typically attach to the house; arbors are freestanding versions. The level of light

an overhead structure filters depends on how closely together the slats are spaced. Covering arbors or pergolas with climbing plants provides additional shade.

Outdoor umbrellas are another option. Look for umbrellas that are sturdy enough not to blow over, but easy to adjust or move.

At certain points in the day, overhead structures might not provide enough shade. Adding a vertical shade or trellis with climbing plants or flowers is one way to block low-angled sunlight.

Privacy

Depending on where you live, privacy may be an important factor in planning your outdoor spaces. Trees, bushes, wood fencing, vine-covered wire fencing, and lattice all provide a measure of privacy. And, as an added benefit, these features help absorb noise from the street or neighbors without completely blocking cooling breezes.

Proper lighting extends the amount of time you can use your outdoor spaces and increases safety at night. Create a flexible lighting scheme with several circuits and switches so you can easily control the amount and location of light.

Lighting

Lighting adds ambience for evening use of spaces while providing safety and security. Exterior lighting may be controlled with a conventional switch, a timer, a photocell (that turns lights on when it gets dark and off when it's light), or motion sensors. Fixtures mounted on exterior house walls may be connected to your home's wiring, while landscape lights will require power from a different source, such as a line-voltage or low-voltage lighting system.

For non-security lights, install switches that you can control both from indoors and outside. Use long-life bulbs, such as energy-saving, outdoor-rated CFLs, which don't need to be changed as often as other bulb types.

Path Lighting Options

Low-voltage or solar-powered fixtures are the easiest options for illuminating walkways. Low-voltage fixtures are safe, inexpensive, and easy to install. They are typically mounted on short stems that direct light downward and work best spaced 8 to 12 feet apart. If your yard gets plenty of sunlight, solar-powered fixtures are an option. They can be installed without digging or wiring and require minimal maintenance, although they typically aren't as bright as other fixtures.

New developments in LED path lighting make it an attractive option. LEDs offer warm, white light much like incandescent bulbs and use very little energy—which means you may be able to go as long as 18 years without having to change the bulbs.

Lighting Options

The ideal outdoor lighting plan combines low-intensity downlighting on poles, trees, roof overhangs, and the side of the house with additional lights positioned low to the ground. On patios or decks, mount lights spaced about 6 feet apart just below seated eye level (about 24 to 36 inches up) to provide even illumination that's easy on the eyes. You can supplement these with portable fixtures, such as battery-powered candle lanterns or lamps.

Extra illumination is necessary for stairs and ramps. Stair lights may be recessed into a post or wall adjacent to the stairs or even inset into stair risers or under the rail.

Use a combination of lighting for walkways as well. Tree-mounted lighting illuminates walkways and reduces shadows. Low-level solar lights may provide enough extra illumination along pathways. There are also special lighting options, such as in-ground lights the same dimensions as standard pavers.

Photo courtesy of Progress Lighting

Deck lights can be mounted on walls, posts, and other surfaces. Look for lights that are hooded to shield the light source and reduce glare. The higher a light is mounted on railings or steps, the more area it will illuminate.

Decks

The style of your house, the location and shape of your yard, and your budget all influence the deck you choose to build. Also consider low-maintenance materials and accessibility in your deck design.

A universally designed deck is durable, easy to maintain, and accessible and includes plenty of room for entertaining or relaxing. To make your deck easily navigable, include an area of open space at least 5 feet in diameter for traffic flow, extra seating for entertaining, and wheelchair turnaround space.

Materials

The surface of your deck should be durable, smooth, level, and free of defects such as cracks or splinters. The space between deck boards should be narrow enough that people don't trip over them, but wide enough to allow for drainage.

When it comes to selecting maintenance-free materials, manufactured decking is a good choice because it is durable and doesn't require much attention aside from occasional cleaning. It is available with a textured, nonslip surface with a wood grain pattern. Options include plastic, vinyl, composite, and rubber.

Hardwood is attractive, although you may need to seal or stain it yearly to preserve the color of the wood. Redwood, cedar, and cypress naturally resist rot and insects. Tropical hardwoods, such as ipe, are popular, too; ipe, a South American species, is impervious to the elements, slip-resistant when wet, insect-resistant, and naturally fire-resistant.

Styles

The deck configuration you build may depend on your budget and the style of house you live in. For instance, a single-level, ranch-style house might look good with a platform-style deck, while a two- or three-story home may be a candidate for a multilevel deck. Think about how easy it will be to access and use your deck. A platform deck is easier to access than a multilevel one with sets of stairs. Common deck styles include the following.

Platform. These single-level decks are built low to the ground, which makes it easy to step into the yard beyond. Check with your

Photo courtesy of DecKorators

A short run of stairs flanked by sturdy railings makes it easy to access the yard beyond this curved deck.

Photo courtesy of DecKorators

Ramp decking should be nonslip. Surfaces made of pressure-treated lumber, synthetic decking, or brushed concrete are common.

Stairs and Ramps

When you design your deck, consider how you'll move between it and the rest of your outdoor spaces. Deck stair design is regulated by strict building codes, so check your local regulations. Be sure to install handrails on each side of the stairway. (See the general stair safety information on pages 24–25.)

A ramp is usable by more people than stairs are and can be an attractive addition—particularly when it matches the style of the deck and is surrounded by landscaping. It's nice to include two handrails on each side of the ramp, one at least 36 inches high for people who are walking and one at 28 inches high for children or people who use wheelchairs. For wheelchair users, a ramp should not have more than 1 inch of rise for every foot of horizontal run. Include a landing for every 3 feet of vertical rise on long ramps so people have a place to stop or turn around. Portable ramps are another option if you have visitors who require one. For more information on ramps, see the "Entrances" section on page 16.

local building department about railing and baluster requirements for different deck heights. If your platform deck doesn't require railings, include a 2-inch-high curb or structures such as benches and planters along the edge to prevent wheels, crutches, canes, or furnishings from slipping off of the deck.

Raised. This style of deck is typically built so it is even with the above-grade first floor of a home. Building codes require railing systems for safety, and you'll need to install stairs or a ramp to provide access to the yard. Surrounding a raised deck with skirting hides framing, prevents large animals from getting under the deck, and allows air to circulate to reduce the chance of mold and moisture damage.

Multilevel. Two-story or multilevel decks, which provide access to the upper levels of the home, work particularly well in yards that have sloping lots. Different areas of this type of deck might be reserved for distinctive functions. To connect multiple levels, you may need to build stairs, walkways, or ramps.

Freestanding. Usually located away from the house, these decks are often positioned close to the ground like platform versions and may not require railings. They can be built to take advantage of the best shade or views in your yard. If your freestanding deck is located away from the house, include a wide walkway or other means of reaching it.

Railings

Railings are an important component of most decks. Railings are built for safety, but they can also enhance the style of your deck. Be sure to build sturdy railings that support at least 250 pounds of weight. Most building codes require that the space between the balusters and rails be no greater than 4 inches and that the space between railing posts not exceed 4 to 6 feet. Horizontal balusters are attractive but should be avoided if you have young children, who may try to use this type of railing as a ladder.

Patios & Courtyards

Key to successful patio design is selecting durable, easy-maintenance materials that create an attractive, smooth surface.

Cost, location, and aesthetics are all factors when it comes to designing a patio that fits your tastes and the style of your home. The most important decision is what materials to use for your patio surface.

Materials

There are a slew of material options available for patios, and each has different characteristics. Some, including certain types of slate, are naturally slip-resistant. Others may be slippery when wet. Bluestone, granite, and quartzite are valued for their hardness and durability.

Research material options in your area to select a paving material that best fits your needs and your climate. In general, look for materials that are low- or no-maintenance, are nonslip, and can be used to create level surfaces that are easy to walk or place furniture on. Avoid handmade tiles, which won't lay flat, and loose materials such as river rock and gravel that don't stay in place when you walk on them.

Stone options worth considering include sandstone, limestone, bluestone, slate, granite, and quartzite. Brick works, too, as long as it is textured and rated for paving and your climate, although it can become slippery when wet. Concrete pavers are available in a variety of colors, sizes, and textures that mimic the look of brick or stone. You may be able to use some forms of ceramic tile as well, as long as they're textured or have a nonslip coating.

A variety of finishing techniques can be used to create texture on concrete patios, which makes them more slip-resistant. Treatments include embedding fine aggregate in the surface, using rock salt to create a pockmarked patina much like travertine, or brushing wet concrete with a straw broom prior to setting.

Think about the colors of the materials you select as well. Light-color paving will brighten a shaded spot, while non-reflective surfaces reduce glare in sunny spots. Some materials store heat more than others; avoid dark

Photo courtesy of Gloster Limited Furniture

A synthetic wicker table and chairs provide a durable, moisture-proof spot for dining outdoors.

A stone patio inset with decorative tiles creates an attractive surface for an outdoor room. It's important to choose nonslip patio materials, especially if the surface isn't shielded from the elements.

If you love alfresco cooking and dining, turn your patio into an outdoor kitchen. Many universal design guidelines for indoor kitchens can be used outdoors.

pavers in warm climates as they absorb heat and may burn bare feet. Color is useful for distinguishing patio borders. You can delineate the edges of your patio by including a border of dyed concrete or stones in a color that contrasts with the rest of the patio.

Design

Patios can be designed in any number of configurations, depending on the shape and slope of your backyard. Of course they are easiest to build and access on a flat stretch of yard next to the house. You can use more than one paving material to differentiate distinctive living areas on your patio; just make certain the transition between the materials is smooth. If steps are necessary, make them deeper than indoor steps and add frequent landings to make climbing easier.

Outdoor Furnishings and Fabrics

Whether you want a dining space for entertaining or intimate seating areas for chatting, furnishings and fabrics add comfort to outdoor spaces.

Outdoor furniture should be sturdy, durable, weatherpoof, and comfortable. Select pieces that fit the style of your outdoor scheme and are easy to move around. Material options include wood, plastic, resin, lightweight aluminum, wrought iron, cast iron, steel, and synthetic wicker.

Cushions upholstered in fabrics designed for outdoor use should resist fading and mildew. Even if they are designed to withstand the elements, bring cushions inside when they're not in use so they last longer.

Pools & Spas

A pool or spa can add fun, exercise, and relaxation to your dream home. With the right materials and landscaping, these features can be accessible, attractive, and not difficult to maintain.

Pools and spas may be prefabricated or custom-made and can be located above- or below-ground depending on your budget and the site. Keep in mind they require access to electrical as well as plumbing systems.

Pools

Easy-access pools are a fun attraction for children and adults of all ages. In addition, pools may be used for exercise or physical therapy. Aquatic athletic equipment ranging from $20 hand-held resistance bars to $3,000 underwater treadmills or swim-in-place jets provide benefits of water exercise even if you don't have space for a large pool.

Safe pool access is important. If you already have a pool, you can make it easier to use by

adding a ramp, lift, or transfer tiers (shallow steps that allow a swimmer who uses a wheelchair to transfer to the upper step and then lower themselves into and out of the pool one step at a time).

With new pools, grading one side of the pool with a gradually sloped floor (often called zero-depth entry) eases the transition. Sloped entries should have a maximum 1:12 pitch and handrails on both sides to provide support for users with limited mobility when entering or exiting the water.

Spas

Like pools, spas can provide physical therapy and relaxation. When filled with water, spas can weigh up to 2 tons, so they require professionally engineered, heavy-duty foundations to support their weight.

When you select a spa, make sure it has at least one accessible entry point. For in-ground spas, the top lip can be close to flush with the patio flooring, which helps ease the transition into the tub. For additional safety, the spa should include handrails, grab bars, and slip-resistant surfaces. Avoid spas with sharp corners or edges. Easy-to-lift covers, top-loading filters, hand controls that can be used from inside or outside the tub, adjustable jets, and wide seats and stairs are worth looking for as well.

Photo courtesy of Blue Haven Pools & Spas

Beautiful landscaping can enhance the appearance of pools and spas, but trees or shrubs that lose their leaves will increase the amount of pool maintenance.

Railings make entering and exiting this pool safer and easier. For even more usability, plan a pool with a gradually sloped floor.

Photo courtesy of Blue Haven Pools & Spas

Surrounding Surfaces

Around a pool or spa, plan for at least 42 to 48 inches of unobstructed surface so there's room to walk or sit. A clear area 5 feet in diameter at one end of the pool provides a spot for setting up patio furniture or wheelchair turnaround space.

Around pools and spas avoid dark patio surfaces that absorb heat (and may burn feet) or slick materials such as glazed ceramic tile and polished marble. Consider edging the patio surface near the pool with a material that contrasts in color and texture with the rest of the patio, so it's easy to tell when you're close to the water.

If you're building a deck around a pool or spa, make sure wood decking materials are weather-resistant and sealed each year.

Shaded areas that overlook the pool but are safely away from the water are best for outdoor seating areas. Choose waterproof furnishings and fabrics.

Photo courtesy of Gloster Furniture Limited

Safety Tip

Most building codes require that pools be surrounded by childproof fences and gates; some codes also require fences around spas. Hot tubs should have covers with childproof latches. Reserve an easy-to-reach spot on a wall or fence nearby for lifesaving devices. And never allow children near a pool or spa unless they are in the presence of an able-bodied adult and are wearing appropriate flotation devices.

Gardens

Flowers and other greenery enhance the appearance of your yard and the value of your home. Gardening can also be a therapeutic activity. With planning, you can make it easy for everyone to access and enjoy the garden.

Low-maintenance groundcovers and other plantings can reduce the amount of time you have to spend caring for your yard. Adding overhead structures adorned with climbing plants can provide shade and reduce glare.

Even people who use wheelchairs or who can't kneel for extended periods of time can tend raised planting beds. If space is limited, or you want to minimize your effort, consider planter boxes. Boxes positioned 24 to 40 inches high on fences, deck railings, or windows are easiest to access. Container gardens (preferably using lightweight pots that are easy to lift or roll) on patios or balconies are also an option.

Drip irrigation systems are efficient and easy to use. If you use regular hoses, look for ones

Photo courtesy of The Able Gardener LLC

This specialized bench allows gardeners to pot plants while standing or sitting and is available in a variety of heights. Ergonomic garden tools make tasks even easier.

that are kink-resistant and not too heavy. Garden spigots ideally should be high enough to eliminate the need for bending and reaching for watering. A hose bib mounted on the wall can make access easier.

To reduce the amount of watering your yard requires, consider xeriscaping. This method, which incorporates drought-tolerant native plants, can create beautiful landscaping that requires minimal attention.

Courtesy of Royal Outdoor Products

Low-maintenance flowerbeds enhance the appearance of a backyard fence. Raise beds to reduce the need for bending and reaching.

Cost Estimates

Exterior Entrance Ramp

An entry ramp makes life easier, not just for a person using a wheelchair, but for anyone who is pushing a stroller, bike, or luggage in and out of the house.

Permanent ramps are more visually appealing than ever, as architects and landscape designers have developed innovative ways to integrate them with a home's architecture and landscaping. If your front entry doesn't allow enough space for a ramp, consider having one installed at a side or back entrance.

Ramp length depends on the height of the door above grade. The maximum slope a person using a manual wheelchair can navigate is 1 inch of rise in 12 inches of run. (For example, a door 18 inches above grade requires a ramp 18 feet long.) For many people, however, this slope is challenging and 1:16 to 1:20 is preferred.

This estimate includes a pressure-treated lumber ramp 15 feet long and 4 feet wide with decorative wood handrails (including balusters and finials). Your project costs will vary based on local economic conditions and availability of contractors.

Estimate Breakdown

Ramp 15 feet long by 4 feet wide, pressure-treated lumber—to include all footings, framing, sealants, and finishes.	$4,800.00
Sub-total	**$4,800.00**
(Add local sales tax for job total)	

Vertical Platform Lift

Where a ramp won't fit, a vertical platform lift might be an alternative. Lifts can be used inside or outside the house. Users roll a wheelchair onto a platform, close a gate, then press a button, similar to an elevator. The maximum lift height is generally 8 feet. An installed unit costs about $11,000. (See page 25 for a photo of a chairlift.)

A white railing helps blend this attractive ramp with the exterior of the home. To assist visitors, include handrails—mounting one at least 36 inches high and another at least 28 inches high is most accessible.

Photo courtesy of Armstrong World Industries, Inc.

Planning Guide

9

Before you begin building or remodeling your dream home, take a few minutes to consider the information presented in this chapter on home safety, the way "green" design complements universal design, and how to work with contractors to ensure quality results. In addition, take a look at the condo and townhome buying checklist, the planning workbook, and the extensive list of resources that follows to help you move closer to your goals for a dream home that will accommodate your needs for a lifetime.

Home Security

Whether you live in the city or a rural area, the risk of crime is a reality. Protect your home and family with these security tactics, which are relatively easy to incorporate into your home.

Many thefts are crimes of opportunity, but burglars also observe and select homes they know will be unoccupied. The following considerations can help reduce your risk.

Security Smarts

- Choose solid-core or metal doors.
- Keep doors and windows locked. Remove or prune trees and shrubbery that provide hiding places near doors and windows.
- Use deadbolt locks. With a key on both sides, an intruder cannot break a side window and reach in to open the door. (Keep the key close to the door for household members, but out of sight from the outside.)
- Choose Grade 1 or Grade 2 locks that stand up to prying, twisting, and picking. Look for a 1-inch throw bolt, a "dead-latch" that will keep the lock from being slipped with a credit card, and beveled casing that will prevent someone from shearing off the lock's cylinder pins with channel-lock pliers. The strike plate should be heavy-duty with four 3-inch screws for a wood door frame. This helps prevent the jamb from being kicked open. A minimum of one long screw should also be used in each door hinge.
- Install a wide-angle 160-degree peephole, mounted at 58 inches or lower as needed.
- Make sure your doorbells can be heard throughout the house so you know when someone is at the door. Rather than having a loud chime, consider placing chimes throughout the home. To accommodate people who have trouble hearing, install lights that flash when the doorbell rings.

- Consider including an intercom answering system with video cameras so you can see who is at the door. With sound transmission, you can communicate with visitors as well. A system that includes a remote control allows you to usher guests in. Some drop-down security monitors even allow you to watch television or listen to music on the same screen.
- Keep your garage door closed and locked.
- Protect sliding glass doors with a piece of wood or metal placed in the track or by screw-down blocking devices. To prevent loose doors from being lifted off the track, keep them adjusted and consider an anti-lift device.
- If you have an alarm system, neighborhood watch organization, or watchdog, post a sign on doors or windows.
- Don't forget lighting—inside and out. Cover all points of entry, areas where intruders could hide, and walkways. Use timers or photocell lights and motion-detector lights.

Photo courtesy of Wellcraft

In addition to security measures, safety considerations are important, too. For instance, window wells that are 44 inches below grade level must have a permanent ladder or steps for egress.

Both green building and universal design aim to create healthier, more comfortable homes—plus green building helps the environment and can lower utility bills.

Green Building

The connection between universal design and environmentally sensitive design is a logical one. Many sustainable, or "green," building materials, such as cork flooring, also improve the comfort of a home. Plus many of these materials and products can improve your health and safety by minimizing contact with allergens and potentially harmful fumes or chemicals. Some environmentally friendly products considerably lower energy and water bills, too, while saving natural resources.

If you're undertaking new home construction, it pays to consider the opportunities for including energy-efficient heating, air-conditioning, and other systems in your home. Even if you're doing modest remodeling, however, a number of environmentally friendly products and materials can be incorporated into your plans, including low-flow faucets, showerheads, and toilets; energy-efficient windows and light fixtures; and natural or recycled materials such as flooring, countertops, and even furniture.

Green Ideas

Some green products may be a bit more expensive than standard ones in terms of initial costs. Others are no more expensive. And many will substantially reduce energy and water use, not to mention improve the quality of life for you and others. Check out these materials and products whenever you're planning to build or remodel:

- ENERGY STAR-rated appliances, lighting, and ceiling fans

Cork flooring is an environmentally friendly building material. It's also great for universally designed homes because it's resilient, so people who stand on it for a length of time don't suffer the back strain that can come from standing on a hard surface.

Photo courtesy of Armstrong World Industries, Inc.

- ENERGY STAR-rated heating, ventilating, cooling, and hot water systems
- Locally made, salvaged, or recycled building materials (such as wood flooring)
- Lumber made from recycled plastic or wood
- Natural, sustainably harvested materials such as bamboo and cork, certified lumber, and recycled or natural-fiber carpeting
- Insulation with no or low levels of pollutants and irritants
- Low-flow plumbing fixtures and faucets
- Low- or no-VOC and formaldehyde-free varnishes, paints, caulk, and glues
- Furniture made from nontoxic materials such as sustainably harvested or recycled wood and wool or cotton
- Fabrics (such as drapery panels) made of nontoxic, natural materials that do not offgas or contain VOCs

Working with Pros

Once you have an idea of your budget and the features you want to include in your home, it's time to enlist the help of qualified professionals to make your dreams a reality.

Depending on your family's current and future needs, you may wish to begin by consulting an occupational therapist who can identify changes that will ensure that your home continues to be comfortable and functional. If your plans include building, remodeling, or retrofitting, it's a good idea to hire professionals who specialize in universal design.

"I would strongly urge someone who wants to build or redo a house to go to a professional rather than trying to do it on their own," says James Joseph Pirkl, FIDSA. "There are no cut-and-dried formulaic solutions. It's something that requires a certain level of knowledge, sensitivity, and background."

Although this book provides an overview of many universal design concepts, it is not a substitute for the experience of a trained professional. Not all of the professionals involved in your project have to be well-versed in universal design, but it's important that at least one has the expertise to guide you and the rest of the team through the process.

Choosing a Contractor

When choosing an architect, contractor, or other professional, look to friends, family, and others who have done similar projects for their recommendations. Some of the organizations listed on pages 154–155 can help you find qualified professionals in your area. Once you identify a list of professionals, arrange a meeting to interview them, see examples of their work, compare approaches and prices, and obtain references. Make sure each professional is fully licensed and insured.

Photo courtesy of Susan Mack, Homes For Easy Living Universal Design Consultants

A professional who specializes in universal design can help you enhance the usability of every room—such as this dining room, which benefits from ample space and light.

After the interviews, narrow your list down to three professionals and request bids from each. Provide each contractor with the same information so you can fairly and thoroughly compare the bids. It's important to base your decisions on more than the final cost—differences in proposed timelines and materials, as well as personality, may factor into your choice.

Once you select the professionals you would like to work with, obtain a detailed written contract that clearly states start date, completion date, acceptable reasons for delay, what building permits are required and who will obtain them, final inspection and "make good" arrangements, the total cost of the project, the amount and due date of each payment, and who is responsible for cleanup and refuse removal.

Before You Buy

Condominiums and townhomes are attractive options for people looking to downsize from larger homes and minimize maintenance. If you are considering moving, use this checklist as a starting point.

Perhaps you've decided to make the move from your current residence to an easier-to-maintain townhouse or condominium. As you begin shopping, keep in mind the equal importance of usability, comfort, and safety.

This checklist is intended as an overview of some of the elements worth assessing during your search. Consider whether you are looking for a home that is move-in ready or if you are willing to make modifications (assuming they are allowed). It is up to you to decide which elements are priorities and what items you can do without. For instance, moving to a townhome or condominium may mean you have to deal with little or no home maintenance, but are you willing to settle for less living and storage space? Think about your future needs as well as your current ones to ensure you make the best decision and select the unit that works best for you.

Common Areas

- ☐ If there are elevators, there is more than one, and they are reasonably sized.
- ☐ Hallways are reasonably wide and well lit.
- ☐ Doorways are at least 36 inches wide.
- ☐ Common areas are welcoming, well-maintained, and well-lit.

Throughout the Home

- ☐ Rooms are large enough to accommodate furnishings and allow space for people to comfortably move around.
- ☐ Hard flooring is nonslip.
- ☐ Carpeting is low-pile and tightly woven.
- ☐ There is plenty of functional, glare-free lighting.
- ☐ Staircases are well-lit, have nonslip flooring, and include railings on each side of the stairwell.
- ☐ Light switches are easy to reach upon entering each room.
- ☐ The home includes access to telephone lines and the Internet.
- ☐ Windows are insulated, and at least one is operable and easy to open in each room.
- ☐ There is plenty of storage including built-in cabinetry and closet space.
- ☐ Thermostats and security controls have large buttons, are easy-to-read, and are illuminated.

Photo © Jupiterimages

An open floor plan and consistent use of flooring materials make it easy to move through this space.

Kitchen

- ☐ The kitchen layout allows for easy movement and includes functional work areas.
- ☐ Countertops, appliances, and cabinets are positioned at a comfortable height; the primary user can easily reach any controls.
- ☐ Faucets are easy to turn on and off.
- ☐ Ground-fault circuit interrupter (GFCI) receptacles are installed throughout the kitchen.
- ☐ Cabinets are easy to open.

Bathrooms

- ☐ If the home has more than one level, at least one full bathroom is located on the main floor.
- ☐ The bathroom layout allows for easy movement between fixtures.
- ☐ Grab bars are installed near the toilet, shower, and bath, or the walls are reinforced to allow for future grab bar installation.
- ☐ The room includes proper ventilation.
- ☐ Sinks and mirrors are positioned at a comfortable height.
- ☐ Faucets are easy to turn on and off.

Other Rooms

- ☐ The laundry area is accessible and on the main floor of the home.
- ☐ Mechanical equipment is located in an area that is secure, yet easy to reach.
- ☐ If a garage is included, it is large enough that there will be plenty of room around any vehicles that you may park there. In addition, the home is easy to enter from the garage.

Exterior

- ☐ The monthly fee covers all exterior maintenance.
- ☐ Walkways to the home or building are wide, even, and well-maintained.
- ☐ Sidewalks include curb cuts for wheelchair access from the parking area.
- ☐ At least one entrance provides stair-free access.
- ☐ Doorways are at least 36 inches wide.
- ☐ Doors include lever-style handles.
- ☐ There is exterior lighting for safety/security.
- ☐ The front door or entrance to the building is covered and well-lit.
- ☐ Parking is easily accessed from the home.
- ☐ The unit (and the entire building if it is a condo) is secure.

Selecting the right townhome should include an assessment of the exterior. Here neatly maintained grounds, a level walkway, and attached garage are all bonuses. The shallow step from the walk to the entrance is maneuverable for many and could accept a small ramp if needed.

Planning Workbook

As a starting point for the planning process and to more fully envision what the rooms in your universally designed home will look like, use the grid and illustrations on these pages to sketch out your ideas.

Copy the grid and illustrations on the following pages to original size and cut out the templates to begin designing the rooms in your home. As you lay out the templates, keep in mind that one square on the grid equals one square foot of floor space. Consider universal design guidelines—particularly in regard to the width of pathways between walls, cabinets, appliances, and furnishings. As you place items in each room, also keep in mind details such as door swings and drawer extensions, which are shown as gray lines on the templates.

Bath

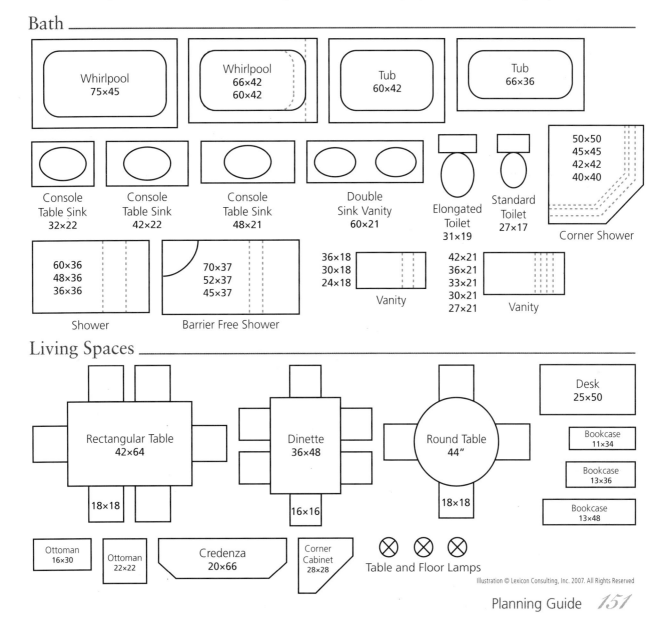

Whirlpool
75×45

Whirlpool
66×42
60×42

Tub
60×42

Tub
66×36

Console
Table Sink
32×22

Console
Table Sink
42×22

Console
Table Sink
48×21

Double
Sink Vanity
60×21

Elongated
Toilet
31×19

Standard
Toilet
27×17

50×50
45×45
42×42
40×40

Corner Shower

60×36
48×36
36×36

Shower

70×37
52×37
45×37

Barrier Free Shower

36×18
30×18
24×18

Vanity

42×21
36×21
33×21
30×21
27×21

Vanity

Living Spaces

Rectangular Table
42×64

Dinette
36×48

Round Table
44"

Desk
25×50

Bookcase
11×34

Bookcase
13×36

Bookcase
13×48

18×18

16×16

18×18

Ottoman
16×30

Ottoman
22×22

Credenza
20×66

Corner
Cabinet
28×28

Table and Floor Lamps

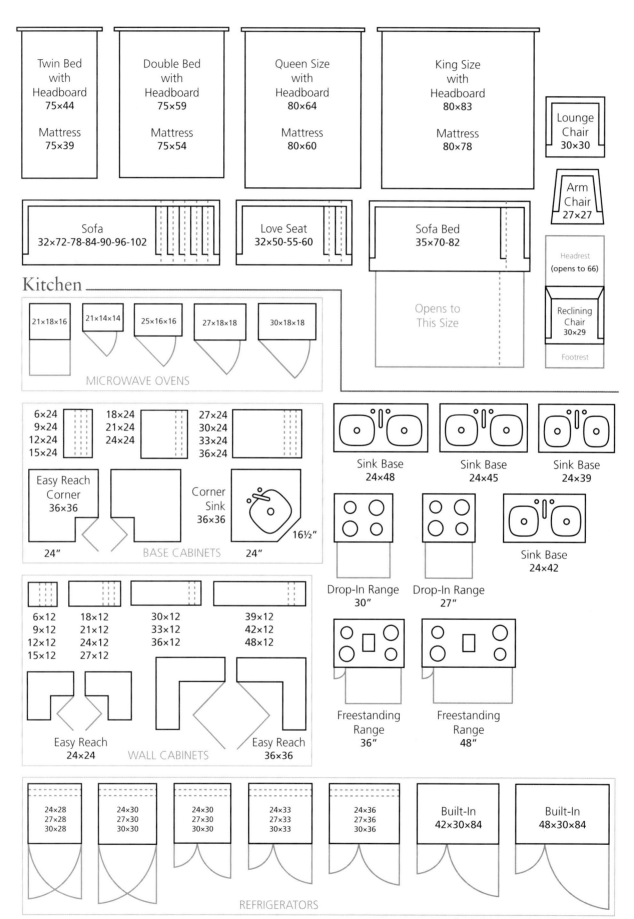

Twin Bed
with
Headboard
75×44

Mattress
75×39

Double Bed
with
Headboard
75×59

Mattress
75×54

Queen Size
with
Headboard
80×64

Mattress
80×60

King Size
with
Headboard
80×83

Mattress
80×78

Lounge
Chair
30×30

Arm
Chair
27×27

Sofa
32×72-78-84-90-96-102

Love Seat
32×50-55-60

Sofa Bed
35×70-82

Opens to
This Size

Headrest
(opens to 66)

Reclining
Chair
30×29

Footrest

Kitchen

21×18×16   21×14×14   25×16×16   27×18×18   30×18×18

MICROWAVE OVENS

6×24
9×24
12×24
15×24

18×24
21×24
24×24

27×24
30×24
33×24
36×24

Easy Reach
Corner
36×36

Corner
Sink
36×36

24"   BASE CABINETS   24"   16½"

Sink Base
24×48

Sink Base
24×45

Sink Base
24×39

Drop-In Range
30"

Drop-In Range
27"

Sink Base
24×42

6×12
9×12
12×12
15×12

18×12
21×12
24×12
27×12

30×12
33×12
36×12

39×12
42×12
48×12

Freestanding
Range
36"

Freestanding
Range
48"

Easy Reach
24×24

WALL CABINETS

Easy Reach
36×36

24×28
27×28
30×28

24×30
27×30
30×30

24×30
27×30
30×30

24×33
27×33
30×33

24×36
27×36
30×36

Built-In
42×30×84

Built-In
48×30×84

REFRIGERATORS

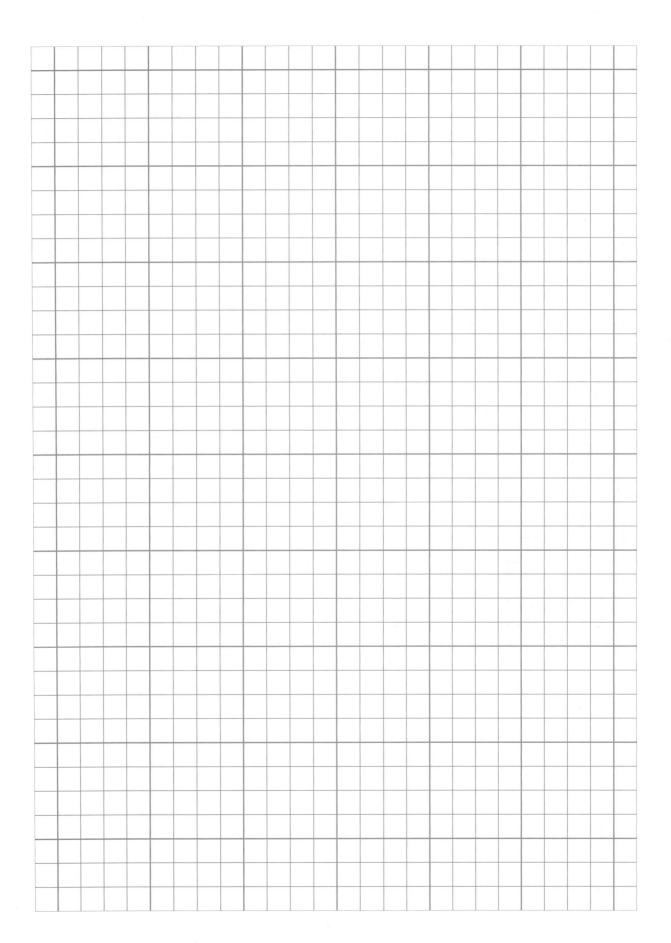

Resources

The following resources provide information on universal design, aging in place, accessibility, assistive technology, building, remodeling, and more. They are provided to give you a starting point for learning more about barrier-free design.

ABLEDATA
Database funded by the federal government that provides information about assistive technology and rehabilitative equipment. 800/227-0216, www.abledata.com

Access Board
Independent federal agency that oversees the ADA Accessibility Guidelines. 202/272-0080, www.access-board.gov

Adaptive Environments
Nonprofit dedicated to promoting access and universal design locally, nationally, and internationally. 617/695-1225, www.adaptenv.org

American Association of Retired Persons (AARP)
Provides resources and publications on aging in place and universal design. The Home Design portion of their website is particularly helpful. 202/434-6049, www.aarp.org

American Society of Interior Designers
Aging in Place Council
Provides information and articles about designing for aging in place and universal design. 202/546-3480, www.asid.org

Center for Inclusive Design and Environmental Access (IDEA)
Dedicated to improving the design of environments and products by making them more usable, safer, and appealing to people with a wide range of abilities throughout their lifespan. 716/829-3485 x329, www.ap.buffalo.edu/idea

The Center for Universal Design
National research, information, and technical assistance center that evaluates, develops, and promotes universal design. 919/515-3082, www.design.ncsu.edu/cud

Certified Aging-in-Place Specialist Program (CAPS)
The NAHB Remodelers, NAHB Research Center, NAHB 50+ Housing Council, and AARP collaborated to develop the CAPS programs to address the growing number of consumers who will soon require home modifications. 800/368-5242, www.nahb.org/caps

Concrete Change
A project of the Statewide Independent Living Council of Georgia. 404/378-7455, www.concretechange.org

EasyLiving Home
The nation's first voluntary certification program that specifies criteria in everyday construction to add convenience in new homes regardless of age, size, or physical ability. www.easylivinghome.org

Independent Living Research Utilization Program
A national center for information, training, research, and technical assistance in independent living. 713/520-0232, www.ilru.org

Iowa State University Department of Human Development and Family Studies
Provides information on universal design, home accessibility, assistive technology, and more. www.extension.iastate.edu/housing

National Association of Home Builders Research Center
Provides information on remodeling strategies developed by the National Center for Seniors' Housing Research. 800/638-8556, www.nahbrc.org

National Council on Independent Living
NCIL advances independent living and the rights of people with disabilities through consumer-driven advocacy. 703/525-3406, www.ncil.org

National Resource Center for Supportive Housing and Home Modifications
A nonprofit organization dedicated to promoting aging in place and independent living. 213/740-6060, www.homemods.org

Shared Solutions America
A national nonprofit organization and resource center for education, technology, and funding alternatives for seniors and people of all ages with disabilities. www.livablehomes.org

The Universal Design Alliance
A nonprofit corporation committed to creating awareness and expanding the knowledge of universal design through education programs, services, and resources. 770/667-4591, www.universaldesign.org

Universal Designers & Consultants, Inc.
Provides universal design information. 301/270-2470, www.universaldesign.com

Building and Remodeling Organizations

American Institute of Architects
202/626-7300, www.aia.org

American Lighting Association
800/605-4448, www.americanlightingassoc.com

American Occupational Therapy Association
301/652-2682, www.aota.org

American Society of Landscape Architects
202/898-2444, www.asla.org

National Association of Home Builders
800/368-5242, www.nahb.org

National Association of the Remodeling Industry
847/298-9200, www.nari.org

National Kitchen and Bath Association
800/843-6522, www.nkba.org

Green Building Resources

Department of Energy
800/342-5363, www.doe.gov/yourhome.htm

ENERGY STAR
888/782-7937, www.energystar.gov

Forest Stewardship Council
202/342-0413, www.fscus.org

U.S. Green Building Council
800/795-1747, www.usgbc.org

Universal Design Products

The following list of universal design products is provided as a starting point for gathering project information. It is not intended to be all-inclusive or an endorsement of any particular products.

Access Control Systems/Keyless Entry
Chamberlain www.chamberlain.com
Marantec www.marantecamerica.com

Adjustable-height Cabinets
AD-AS www.ad-as.com
Alno AG www.alno.com

Automated Retractable Awnings
Somfy www.somfy.com
SunSetter www.sunsetter.com

Deck Lighting
SPJ Lighting, Inc. www.spjlighting.com
SwiftDeck www.swiftdeck.com

Elevators & Chair Lifts
National Wheel-O-Vator Co., Inc. www.wheelovator.com
ThyssenKrup Access www.tkaccess.com

Gardening Tables and Raised Planters
The Able Gardener www.theablegardener.com
Simple Gardens www.simplegardens.com

Hands-Free Faucets
Delta faucets www.deltafaucet.com
EZ Faucet www.ezfaucet.com

LED Path Lighting
LED Waves www.ledwaves.com
Sylvania www.sylvania.com

Lifting-Seat Chairs
Golden Technologies www.goldentech.com
Pride Mobility Products www.pridemobility.com

Lighting, Whole-Home and Dimmers
Leviton www.leviton.com
Lutron Electronics, Inc. www.lutron.com

Modular Ramps
AlumiRamp www.alumiramp.com
EZ-Access® www.ezaccess.com

Personal Emergency Response Systems (PERS)
AlertOne www.alert-1.com
Life Station www.lifestation.com

Pop-up Shelves/Pull-out Cabinets
Armstrong www.armstrong.com
KraftMaid Cabinetry www.kraftmaid.com

Scald Guards for Faucets
Delta Faucets www.deltafaucet.com
H2otStop www.h2otstop.com

Specialty Kitchen Drawers
GE www.GEAppliances.com
U-Line Corporation www.u-line.com

Stairlifts
Acorn Stairlifts www.acornstairlifts.com
Ameriglide www.ameriglide.com

Telephone Systems with Visual Ringers
Clarity www.clarityproducts.com
GE www.home-electronics.net

Underwater Treadmill and Jet/Resistance Therapy
HydroWorx www.hydroworx.com
Recreonics www.recreonics.com

Walk-in Bathtubs
DCE Bathing Systems www.walkintub.com
USA Tubs www.usatubs.com

Window Accessibility Retrofit Kits
Window Ease www.windowease.com

Credits

The following professionals kindly contributed their expertise to the research and writing of this book. In addition, the companies listed on these pages generously supplied most of the photography used in the book.

Professionals

Susan Mack, OTR/L, NAHB/CAPS
President, Homes for Easy Living Universal
Design Consultants
760/409-7565, **www.homesforeasyliving.com**

Mary Jo Peterson, CKD, CBD, NAHB/CAPS
President, Mary Jo Peterson, Inc
203/775-4763, **www.mjpdesign.com**

James Joseph Pirkl, FIDSA
Founding Director,
Transgenerational Design Matters, Inc.
505/821-9221, **www.transgenerational.org**

Kasey K. Thompson, Pharm.D.
Director, Patient Safety
American Society of Health System
Pharmacists
www.ashp.org

Eunice Noell-Waggoner, L.C.
President, Center of Design for an
Aging Society
503/292-2912, **www.centerofdesign.org**

In addition to recognizing the above professionals for their contributions, we would like to thank **The Center for Universal Design** for their expert review of this book.

Photo Credits

ALNO USA
One Design Center Place #634
Boston, MA 02210
617/896-2700
www.alno.com

Andersen Corporation
800/426-4261
www.andersenwindows.com

Armstrong World Industries, Inc.
717/397-0611
www.armstrong.com

Baldwin Hardware Corporation
800/566-1986
www.baldwinhardware.com

Blue Haven Pools & Spas
75 U.S. offices
800/961-7946
www.bluehaven.com

California Closet Co. Inc.
800/274-6754
www.californiaclosets.com

ClosetMaid.com
www.closetmaid.com

Conrad Shades
Conrad Imports, Inc.
600 Townsend Street
Suite 400W
San Francisco, CA 94103
866/426-6723
info@conradshades.com
www.conradshades.com

DecKorators
50 Crestwood Executive Center
Suite 308
Crestwood, MO 63126
800/332-5724
info@deckorators.com
www.deckorators.com

Dunn-Edwards Corporation
4885 East 52nd Place
Los Angeles, CA 90040
888/DE-PAINT
www.dunnedwards.com

Fabrica
2801 Pullman Street
Santa Ana, CA 92705
800/854-0357
www.fabrica.com

General Electric Company
800/626-2005
www.geappliances.com

Gloster Furniture Limited
uk@gloster.com
www.gloster.com

Great Grabz
Abbie Joan Enterprises
4535 Domestic Ave. Ste D
Naples, FL 34104

GROHE America, Inc.
241 Covington Drive
Bloomingdale, IL 60108
630/582-7711
info@groheamerica.com
www.groheamerica.com

Hy-Lite Products, Inc.
1011 Park Lane
Greensboro, GA 30642
800/423-3032
www.hy-lite.com

IKEA
877/345-4532
www.ikea.com

Independent Living USA
Walk-In Bathtub Specialists
800/403-7409
info@usatubs.com
www.independentlivingusa.com
www.usatubs.com

JELD-WEN Windows & Doors
800/877-9482
www.jeld-wen.com

Kohler Co.
www.kohler.com

KraftMaid Cabinetry
P.O. Box 1055
15535 South State Ave.
Middlefield, OH 44062
888/562-7744
www.kraftmaid.com

Lasco Bathware
8101 East Kaiser Blvd., Suite 200
Anaheim, CA 92808
714/993-1220
www.lascobathware.com

Mannington Mills, Inc.
800/482-9527
www.mannington.com

Mascord
Alan Mascord Design Associates, Inc.
1305 NW 18th Avenue
Portland, OR 97209
800/411-0231
customerservice@mascord.com
www.mascord.com

Moen Incorporated
25300 Al Moen Drive
North Olmsted, OH 44070
800/321-8809
www.moen.com

Mohawk Flooring
800/2MOHAWK
www.mohawk-flooring.com

Prairie View Industries
P.O. Box 575
2620 Industrial Drive
Fairbury, NE 68352
800/554-7267
(fax) 402/729-4058
info@pviramps.com
www.pviramps.com

Pressalit Care
5B David Drive
Essex Junction, VT 05452
800/401-7008
usa@pressalitcare.com

Progress Lighting
www.progresslighting.com

Quick-Step Inc.
7834 C.F. Hawn Freeway
Dallas, TX 75217
888/387-9882
www.quick-step.com

Robern
701 N. Wilson Ave.
Bristol, PA 19007
800/877-2376
customersupport@robern.com
www.robern.com

Royal Outdoor Products
877/GO ROYAL (467-6925)
www.royaloutdoor.com

Savaria Concord Lifts Inc.
4150 Highway #13, Laval
Quebec, Canada
H7R 6E9
800/931-5655
savaria@savaria.com

Sherwin-Williams
www.sherwin-williams.com

Snaidero
877/SNAIDERO
www.snaidero.com

Smarthome
16542 Millikan Avenue
Irvine, CA 92606
800/762-7846
www.smarthome.com

STAINMASTER
800/438-7668
www.stainmaster.com

Stroheim
30-30 47th Avenue
Long Island City, NY 11105
800/974-8444
www.stroheim.com

Sub-Zero Freezer Company
800/222-7820
www.subzero.com

Sunbrella
Glen Raven Custom Fabrics, LLC
1831 North Park Avenue
Glen Raven, NC 27217
336/221-2211
www.sunbrella.com

Susan Mack
Homes for Easy Living
Universal Design Consultants
760/409-7565
www.homesforeasyliving.com

The Able Gardener LLC
Gene Rothert
www.theablegardener.com

The Shade Store
800/754-1455
www.theshadestore.com

Thibaut Inc.
800/223-0704
www.thibautdesign.com

Travis Industries
4800 Harbour Pointe Blvd. S.W.
Mukilteo, WA 98275
800/654-1177
www.travisproducts.com

Valcucine
Via L. Savio 11
33170 Pordenone (Italy)
Tel. +39 0434 517 911
Fax +39 0434 517 933
info@valcucine.it
www.valcucine.it

VELUX America Inc.
450 Old Brickyard Road
P.O. Box 5001
Greenwood, SC 29648
800/888-3589
www.veluxusa.com

Viking
111 Front Street
Greenwood, Mississippi 38930
888/VIKING1
www.vikingrange.com

Weather Shield® Windows & Doors
800-477-6808
www.weathershield.com

Wellcraft Egress Windows
and Window Wells
888/812-9545
www.wellcraftwells.com

Wilsonart International, Inc.
2400 Wilson Place
P.O. Box 6110
Temple, TX 76503
www.wilsonart.com

Index